A Handbook for Writing Skills

A HANDBOOK FOR WRITING SKILLS

Naana Jane Opoku-Agyemang
*Lecturer, Department of English,
University of Cape Coast, Cape Coast*

GHANA UNIVERSITIES PRESS
ACCRA
1998

Published by
Ghana Universities Press
P. O. Box 4219
Accra

© Naana Jane Opoku-Agyemang 1998

ISBN: 9-9643020-10

Acknowledgements
We are grateful to the underlisted publishers for their permission to reprint illustrative materials from their publications thus:
Addison Wesley Longman Limited for material taken from Hay, Margaret J. and Sharon Stitcher (Eds) 1987. *African Women South of the Sahara*; George Allen and Unwin Limited for material taken from Oppong, Christine (Ed.) 1983. *Female and Male in West Africa;* and The North-South Institute for material taken from McNicoll, Andre 1983. *Drug Trafficking: A North-South Perspective.*

Produced in Ghana
Typesetting by Ghana Universities Press, Accra
Printing and binding by Assemblies of God Literature Centre, Accra

*For
Mansa
My Sister and My Friend*

CONTENTS

Preface	x
Chapter 1 READING	1
Introduction	1
Where do I Read	2
How do I Read	2
Habits which Lead to Slow Reading	3
Reading the Paragraph	3
Skimming the Paragraph	4
Scanning the Paragraph	4
The Topic Sentence	4
Reading the Chapter	11
Review the Chapter	12
Revise the Chapter	12
Reading the Textbook	13
The Title Page	13
Author's Name	14
Reading the Table of Contents	15
Reading the Preface	20
Reading the Index	22
Chapter 2 NOTE-MAKING AND NOTE-TAKING	24
Taking Notes from Lectures	24
The Outline	25
The Summary	25
Making Notes from Reading	26
Chapter 3 BASIC SENTENCE PATTERNS	30
Subject-Verb Complement	31
Subject-Verb-Object-Complement	32
Subject-Verb-Object-Adverb	33
Subject-Verb-Object-Object	33
Introduction	35
Coordination	35
Relating Equal Ideas through Coordination	35
Addition	36
Contrast	36
Choice	36
Result	37

Faulty Coordination	37
Exercises on Coordination	38
Subordination	42
Condition	45
Result or Purpose	46
Reason or Cause	47
Exercises on Subordination	48

Chapter 4 SUBJECT-VERB AGREEMENT 53
Exercises on Subject-Verb Agreement 58

Chapter 5 AMBIGUITIES AND DANGLING MODIFIERS 64
Ambiguities	64
Ambiguity in Noun Clusters	65
Ambiguity in Verb Clusters	66
Some Exercises on Ambiguities	67
More Exercises on Ambiguities	68
Ambiguity in Pronouns	71
Further Exercises on Ambiguities	73
Dangling Modifiers	77
How to Avoid Dangling Modifiers	78
Exercises on the Dangling Modifier	79
More Exercises on the Dangling Modifier	81

Chapter 6 THE ACADEMIC ESSAY 84
Introduction	84
The Topic	84
The Introduction	87
The Outline for Essay	88

Chapter 7 PARAGRAPHING 102
Patterns of Development	107
The Direct Pattern	107
Exercise on the Paragraph	109

Chapter 8 COMPOSING THE INTRODUCTION AND THE CONCLUSION 113
The Introduction	113
Illustrations of the Introduction	116
The Conclusion	118

Chapter 9 PUNCTUATION 122
Comma (,)	122
Exercises on the Comma	125

Semi-colon (;)	126
Exercises on the Semi-colon	127
Colon (:)	128
Exercises on the Colon	128
Quotation Marks (" " Or ' ')	129
Exercises on the Comma and Quotation Marks	130
Apostrophe (')	131
Exercises on the Apostrophe	132
Question Mark (?)	133
Exercises on the Question Mark	133
Parenthesis ( )	133
Exercises on the Parenthesis	134
Full Stop or Period (.)	134

Chapter 10   DOCUMENTATION; FOOTNOTES AND BIBLIOGRAPHY   135

Footnotes	135
Format for the Footnote	136
Using the Explanatory Footnote	137
Endnotes	137
Exercises on Footnotes and Endnotes	138
The Bibliography	138
Books	140
Magazines, Periodicals, Newspapers	141
Encyclopedias and Almanacs	141
Exercises on the Bibliography	142

Bibliography   145

PREFACE

Those of us who teach in institutions of higher learning often make the assumption that the candidate who qualifies for admission into our institutions is qualified to cope with all the demands of our programmes of study. Experience has shown that, whereas the student may be very competent in his subject of study there might be a deficiency in those areas that hardly any discipline takes on as a direct responsibility.

This handbook has been written to act as a guide towards helping the student who is anxious to take out some of the known frustrations of tertiary education. The book is based on a five-year research carried out with undergraduate students at the University of Cape Coast, where I have been teaching in the Communicative Skills Programme. My sampling reading of student examination answers from the University of Ghana, the University of Science and Technology as well as the then Advanced Teachers Training College at Winneba confirmed the need for such a book.

The handbook is divided into ten chapters. The first two deal with study skills such as reading and making notes. Chapters three and four make suggestions about sentence formation and the basic agreement between subject and verb. While chapter five encourages the formation of both grammatically correct and logically plausible sentences, chapter six introduces the student to the broad demands of the academic essay. In chapters seven and eight detailed attention is paid to writing paragraphs and also introductions and conclusions. Chapter nine deals with the mechanics of writing while chapter ten offers a format for documentation.

This handbook is not to teach students how to write model essays. It shows students how they can improve upon their own writing so that in the end the best of their compositions will be enhanced.

Perhaps this handbook could have come with more exercises than it does, but I hope that the few exercises provided will urge the teacher on to create more exercises for his students, and the students to take very seriously the suggestions about transferring the advice given in the course of the book on to practice.

I could definitely not have written this handbook within the time I did without the opportunity to spend the Spring Quarter, 1993, at Eastern Washington University where I was a visiting faculty member. I was able to take the time off because my husband, and colleague Kwadwo Opoku-Agyemang, gave me the necessary encouragement and support by adding my teaching schedule at the University of Cape Coast onto his own, and by taking over my family responsibilities. I am also grateful to Dr. Felix Boateng, Director,

Black Education Programme, Eastern Washington University, for arranging for me to have a lap-top computer at my disposal, for actually doing some of the editing and for showing enthusiasm about the work. And to Professor J. deG Hanson, Department of Classics, University of Cape Coast, I express my deepest gratitude for his encouragement, thorough reading of the typescript and for the very useful suggestions which he made.

Cape Coast *Naana Jane Opoku-Agyemang*
July, 1993

Chapter 1

READING

Introduction

It is not unusual for the average freshman or woman to complain about the amount of reading required of him/her. In a survey conducted on a sampling of the year groups in one of the halls of residence at the University of Cape Coast, it was revealed that most of the respondents were not very excited by the volume of reading material they are supposed to cover. In the lecture theatre situation the lecturer is invariably greeted by groans when he demands of students to consult a source or two for the purposes of the course. In desperation the students demand almost immediately the number of pages that article they are supposed to read covers. The number of pages determines their readiness or otherwise to read.

As the first year student adviser of my department I have had several occasions to encourage flagging students whose main problem is coping with reading. The euphoria over admission quietly wanes and sometimes the students hover on the borders of despair. One student had even wanted to drop out because he did not see how he could cover the "long" list he was supposed to read in one course. Obviously this student had come to feel that the University was the wrong place for him.

If you have ever felt this mixture of hope and apprehension as a student, or if the euphoria you feel about your admission to a tertiary institution is obliquely marred by confusion over what is expected of you as an undergraduate, or if someone has frightened you about the magnitude of university studies, then read on, closely.

The first and indispensable step is for you to acquire a good dose of confidence. You must believe that you can make a difference in the rate at which you have been reading, that you can read faster and more effectively than you have been doing, and indeed that you can discover, the pleasures of reading the textbook.

What are required are three things:

1. The desire to improve upon your reading.
2. The willingness to make the effort at reading.
3. The discipline of constant practice at reading.

We should practice reading everyday because reading, contrary to being an innate habit, is a skill which is honed to perfection through constant practice. In other words, you have to go beyond complaining about the amount of reading you are supposed to do, and beyond merely wishing you could read faster to actually applying yourself constantly to a method of reading which would enable you to gather the meaning off the printed page with the least effort and within the shortest possible time.

Before we can attain the desired level of proficiency and speed we need to know what to do. The method I am going to introduce will require of you to read at a slower rate than you have been doing; initially this very slow rate is important in helping you to read in a certain way. You will build your speed as you practice and you will soon discover that you are better able to retain the information you are reading than you did previously.

Ask yourself a few questions and attempt to answer them.

Where do I Read?

The atmosphere in which we read has important implications for the amount we retain and the grounds we cover. Some of us may insist that we read better when we lie in bed. So long as the book does not become a sleeping tablet and so long as we can make notes best when we lie down we can continue to read in bed. Others insist that they concentrate better when the music is turned very high. I think this method is very practical if we live on an island all by ourselves. If you have a roommate or live on a floor of a university hall of residence then consideration for others would dictate that you use earphones, at the very least. If you fall into the category of students who read best in a quiet environment then the libraries on the campus will be the best place for you. The location you choose for your reading must be well-ventilated, well-lit and in a pleasant surrounding.

The location for reading is very important because reading demands concentration. Whether in a noisy or quiet place we need direct our attention to the printed page, and for this reason loud music may not appear to create the best environment. Again, since we are concerned with attention, we need to eliminate a lot of activities before we read our textbooks. For example, it is that rare student who can listen to loud music, chat with his roommate, warm a pot of stew and read effectively at the same time.

How do I Read?

Most of us pick up our textbooks and attempt to read from cover to cover. We have been doing that for so long that we have come to assume this practice to be the best. But there is a better way to read a book than from the first word through to the last. You have to read for the purposes of studying. We shall go into the details shortly.

Habits which Lead to Slow Reading

1. Some readers believe they have to read aloud to themselves if they are to remember the contents of the reading material. Acceptable method if you are on the beach by yourself. Terrible method if you either intend to study in the library, or indeed in any environment which includes other people.
2. Lisping the words can be just as irritating to others as reading aloud. Reading involves the eyes and the mind; as a result, a good amount of concentration is indispensable. This reason explains why we may not distract others, if not ourselves, from gathering the meaning off the pages we have to cover in our reading. Apart from this reason, the habit of audibly pronouncing the words while reading makes for slow reading.
3. Some of us read in a fashion which recalls the class one teacher pointing to one word at a time with a cane. Surely it has been almost two decades since class one for most of you, and reading words in isolation at this level interferes with the co-ordination between the eyes and the brain. It also destroys the relationship established between the words which together make up the content of the material. For example:

    (a) This   is   how   a   slow   reader   proceeds.
    (b) While the faster reader   always proceeds   this way.
    Therefore, instead of reading words in isolation, as in (a) above you should read by the eyeful as in (b).

4. It is important to look up key words in your chapter. If you have to look up every other word on the page then the assumption is that the reading is far above your level of competence, and that you are going to proceed at an unacceptably slow rate.

Reading the Paragraph

Graphically, the paragraph is shown in the page either by an indentation on the first line to the left side of the margin or by leaving spaces between blocks of writing. These indentations and spaces serve as important signposts in print or in writing. Good writers do not begin paragraphs because the previous one appears to be too long. The signposts point to the beginning of a new topic or idea for discussion in the article or chapter.

I am aware that it sounds almost ridiculous that we should isolate the paragraph for close study. This is because no one is ever likely to send you to the library to read a single paragraph. However, it is important to acquire the right tools for reading the paragraph because the article or chapter which you are likely to read consists of a string of paragraphs. Usually, the number of paragraphs in an article would coincide with the number of ideas discussed in that piece of writing.

Skimming the Paragraph

It is important to consider, in a cursory manner (skim), the characteristics of the paragraph you are studying. In other words, it might be useful to consider ways of reading the paragraph other than starting from the first word to the last. Skimming the paragraph allows you to isolate words or phrases, in italics, those presented in boldface or isolated on the printed page by some other mechanical means. It is important to understand how these words and phrases would relate directly to your course.

As a student in a tertiary institution, you are not likely to find that small pocket dictionary very useful. The best dictionary to consult is the one in your subject area. For example, a dictionary of sociology or economics will be useful to the social science student. While a dictionary of literary terms will prove invaluable to the student of literature and language. In the same vein the medical student will earn very little by consulting the Oxford Advanced Dictionary. The student will do better to consult a dictionary of anatomy, for example. Always go to your reading armed with such an explanatory source because it would offer you a more comprehensive definition of the vocabulary used in your subject area than would a good, general dictionary, or encyclopedia.

Scanning the Paragraph

Having skimmed the paragraph, the next stage is to examine the paragraph very closely (scan) in order to isolate the main idea being discussed and the relationships which exist between the various sentences in the paragraph. Scanning is important because it allows the reader to determine the main idea being discussed in the paragraph (topic noun) and which sentences are amplifying that idea directly (major supports). Sentences which aid in further explaining the major support sentences are called the minor support sentences.

The Topic Sentence

The topic sentence contains one word or sometimes a group of words around which the paragraph revolves. This sentence is usually placed at the head of the paragraph. In other words, the first sentence of every paragraph is very important. It is possible to isolate that word (not by underlining unless you own the book) and discover what the other sentences are saying about that word. If it is a good paragraph, all the sentences should say something about that word. Some of the sentences speak more directly to that word or help you to understand that word better than others. These sentences are said to be lending major support to the topic noun. Others which do not throw such direct light on the topic noun are called minor support. Also, beware of dud sentences. These are the sentences which appear to help with the topic sentence but indeed are so irrelevant that you can remove them from he paragraph and feel no loss. Let us consider this paragraph together.

Read this Paragraph Carefully

"Religion" brings to mind various images for different people. For some it means belief in God or bowing one's head for prayer. For others it means meditating, with eyes almost closed. For still others religion means an argument over the meaning of "revelation". According to some it means superstition, or at least "traditional views". In a large measure, the possibility, the importance and the way of studying the religious life of man depend on an individual's experience with what he labels religion (F. J. Streng, 1969). *Understanding Religious Man.* California: Dickenson Publishing Company Inc., Belmont.

What is that single topic or idea with which the paragraph is concerned? Can you identify a word in the passage around which hedges the essence of the paragraph? You can answer these two questions by reading the passage slowly, and stringing out this passage, sentence after sentence. Let us consider the first sentence: "Religion brings to mind various images for different people". What subject is the sentence discussing? Can you identify the noun which describes this subject? Obviously the sentence is taking about the subject of religion. If you agree, and you own this book, then underline the word 'religion', preferably with a coloured pen or feltpen. Read the subsequent sentences and find other references made to this noun. After this exercise your paragraph should look like this:

1. *Religion* brings to mind various images to different people.
2. For some *it* means belief in God or bowing one's head for prayer.
3. For others *it* means meditating, with eyes almost closed.
4. For still others religion means an argument over the meaning of *revelation.*
5. According to some it means superstition, or at best *tradtional views.*

6. In a large measure, the possibility, importance, and the way of studying the religious life of man depend on an individual's experience with what he labels *religion.*

Repeat paragraph, this time with italicized words.

We will now isolate each sentence in order to determine its function in relation to the topic noun, 'religion,'

(a) *Sentence one:*

Religion brings to mind various images to different people.

This sentence merely states a fact about religion, that different people bring to bear on the subject different conceptions.

(b) *Sentence two:*

For some it means belief in God or bowing one's head in prayer

This sentence is a major support sentence because it helps in a very direct way to explain what is meant by different conceptions of religion as suggested in sentence one. Here, a specific way of defining religion is provided: a belief in God or a religious activity.

(c) *Sentence three:*

For others it means meditating, with eyes almost closed.

This sentence elaborates on the religious activity provided in sentence two by offering another example of religious activity. In this respect, sentence three acts as a minor support to the topic sentence because it derives from sentence two.

(d) *Sentence four:*

For still others religion means an argument over the meaning of "relevation".

This sentence does offer an example or illustration to the previous two sentences. In this respect, it acts as a minor support by elaborating on what has been suggested in sentences two and three. Here, others understand religion to be an argument.

(e) *Sentence five:*

> According to some it means superstition or at best "traditional views"

This sentence gives yet another example of what religion means to other people.

(f) *Sentence six:*

> In a large measure, the possibility importance, and the way of studying the religious life of man depend on an individual's experience with what he labels religion.

This sentence acts as a summary of the paragraph, by stating the idea suggested in sentence one that religion is conceived of differently by different people. In this respect, it lends major support to sentence one.

Now, using the topic noun as the subject, can you write a single sentence which sums up the essence of the paragraph? You may have a summary sentence like:

> Religion means different things to different people.

This exercise needs a lot of practice but it is useful in reading effectively and in gathering facts for note-making. In the next chapter we shall concern ourselves with making notes. But before then here are a few exercises for you.

Here are the instructions:

1. Read the paragraph.
2. Isolate the topic noun. Underline it if you own this book and also underline all subsequent references made to this noun.
3. In one clear summary, using the topic noun as the subject of the sentence, sum up the paragraph in one sentence.

> The nervous system controls the muscles as it makes use of the skeletal apparatus; it controls the beating of the heart, respiration, and circulation of

the blood. It regulates the secretions of the glands. Therefore this third system, the neural mechanism, rules over the mechanical and chemical integrators that we have just considered. The great gain to the organism through possessing a nervous system is that this system provides the basis for complex and modifiable action, for learning as a result of experience, and for increased adaptability to variety in the environment. So important is the nervous system that most of the remainder of this chapter will be devoted to it. (Hilgard, Ernest R. 1962, *Introduction to Psychology*, New York: Harcourt, Bruce and World Inc.)

The topic noun is ....

The summary sentence is ....

....

....

Probably the main objective of the accounting function is the calculation of profits earned by a business or the losses incurred by it. The earning of profit is after all usually the main reason why the business was set up in the first place, and the proprietor will want to know for various reasons how much profit has been made. First, he will want to know how the actual profits compare with the profits he had hoped to make. He may also want to know his profits for such diverse reasons as: to assist him to plan ahead, to help him to obtain a loan from a bank or from a private individual, to show to a prospective partner or to a person to whom he hopes to sell the business, or maybe he will need to know his profits for income tax purposes. (Wood, Frank, 1984, *Business Accounting* Vol.1, London: Pitman Publishing).

The topic noun is ....

The summary sentence is ....

....

....

While confined here in the Birmingham jail, I came across your recent statement calling my present activities "unwise and untimely". Seldom do I pause to answer criticism of my work and ideas. If I sought to answer all the criticisms that cross my desk, my secretaries would have little time for anything other than such correspondence in the course of the day, and I would have no time for constructive work. But since I feel that you are men of genuine goodwill and that your criticisms are sincerely set forth, I want to try to answer your statement in what I hope will be patient and reasonable terms. (Martin Luther King Jr., "Letter from Birmingham Jail.")

The topic noun is ....

The summary sentence is ....

....

....

Style is the literary equivalent of the differences in appearances and character that distinguish one man from another. Style is partly an expression of the writer's personality, but it is also conditioned by historical influences, literary training, and academic background. Both Milton and Bunyan have something in common because they belong to the same period, but different backgrounds and personalities make their styles quite dissimilar.

The topic noun is ....

The summary sentence is ....

....

....

In a very broad sense, agriculture is the science and art of systematic production of useful plants and animals for man's use through concerted human management. The term has frequently been used interchangeably with farming. While such usage may be quite in order, agriculture embraces more than farming. Agriculture includes farming which means the production of plants and animals on the farms, and goes further to apply also to the application of basic scientific knowledge for better production and to the areas of processing and marketing of farm products. (Adjayi, E.E. & Ekong, E.E. 1981, *General Agriculture and Soils*, London: The Camelot Press Ltd.)

The topic noun is ....

The summary sentence is ....

....

....

West Africans have always exhibited a high tendency to migrate; the various types of population movements historically serve as a means to restore ecological balance and achieve better condition of living and are, in most cases, related to the search for more food, better shelter and greater security. Thus, population movement in West Africa is not a new phenomenon; the region experienced various kinds of population distribution and redistribution centuries before exposure to Western influence. Movements took the form of group migration; however, as the society became more differentiated and the economy increasingly diversified, the motivation for migration became complex; subsequently, the direction of migration altered, becoming more voluntary and economically motivated rather than political or forced. This pattern has been parallelled by a shift from group migration, which characterized the era of internecine warfare, to individual movements; consequently, the migrants' characteristics and motivation became differentiated by socio-economic and demographic features, especially age, sex, occupation and education.

The topic noun is ....

The summary sentence is ....

....

....

You may very well wonder how you are ever going to read an entire chapter if you must isolate each paragraph and apply the above method to it. Our concern in the next section is to discover a method for reading the chapter, and hopefully some of these concerns will be addressed. The questions of speed is very important in the sense that the beginning of most skill-oriented programmes can be trying. You may here recall the first time you handled a needle and string or thread, or tried your hand at the typewriter or even tried to hit a tennis ball. The initial frustrating attempts gave way as you applied yourself more diligently to the methodology suggested, and built up your speed and confidence. You need PRACTICE, and a lot of it. As you progress you will find out that you are spending less and less time completing the exercises.

Reading the Chapter

Introduction
Every so often your instructor sends you to the library to read a chapter or two in a recommended book. What some of you have been doing is to locate the book, turn to the first page of the article and read through to the end. The suggestion here is that there is a more effective way of reading the chapter than you have been doing.

> *Step I*
> Read the title of the chapter very carefully. Make sure you understand the words in it, clearly. For a source, do use a dictionary in your subject area, as I have suggested in the section on 'Read the Paragraph'. The title will give you a good idea of what the entire chapter is about.

> *Step II*
> Survey the chapter by looking out for sub-headings and trying to understand the terms and words used in the sub-heading. You must also look out for maps, charts, illustrations or diagrams. Spend a few minutes trying to understand the keys to these signposts. If there are any words in bold face or highlighted by other mechanical means try to understand them. To read the chapter without first surveying it is to read without purpose, and chances are that you always have to read that same chapter about three times in order to sift out the meaning, because such reading is easily forgotten. In order to approach reading intelligently, expertly and to save a lot of time and frustration, you must survey the chapter.

> *Step III*
> Read the last paragraph of the chapter after the survey. This is important because the last paragraph will offer a summary of the ideas raised in the chapter. Together with the survey and a clear understanding of the title, you may proceed from the first sentence of the chapter; you are now armed with a good idea of what the chapter is all about.

You may even formulate some questions and anticipate some answers, based on the survey you have done.

> *Step IV*
> As you now read on, do bring to bear on the chapter what you have learnt in the previous section on reading the paragraph. Remember that the chapter is a string of paragraphs. Locate the topic noun at every

step and try to sum up the paragraph in a sentence. If the article contains twenty paragraphs and covers nine pages, you will have for notes only twenty sentences which capture the gist of the chapter.

Step V

You are about 75 percent through reading the chapter. If you are the average student you would assume that your work ends with reading the last word and maybe writing out the number of sentences to correspond to the number of paragraphs.

The next 25 percent concerns itself with ensuring that you have actually understood your reading and that you can remember the details without too much trouble.

Review the Chapter

You must give the chapter a final, comprehensive review which should include a close re-examination of the title, the sub-headings, and a close reading of the first and last paragraphs. With the help of your summary sentences write out what you believe the author has discussed in the chapter.

Revise the Chapter

Read the introduction to the chapter again and close the page, or better still use a page marker. Try to recall what the introduction proposed to discuss in the page. Use your notebook and jot down the points as you remember them. Read the paragraph again and find out how many of the points you have written down in your notebook. You can rate your ability – recall through this method of revision. Apply this method to as many paragraphs as possible, and always check your success rate. Remember that there is no better known method of improving upon a skill than practice. Open a chapter in the textbook of one of your subjects – try to apply steps I–V. There is no point just reading what I am telling you. Apply it constantly and find out for yourself whether the method is useful or not.

You are almost at the end of the methodology proposed for reading the chapter. Before we close that chapter we must consider collateral reading. At the end of most chapters in textbooks you will find a list of reading materials under the heading 'References', 'Bibliography', 'Suggested Reading', 'Further Reading' or some such title. This section contains references to material which may either have been used in the course of the discussion which forms the chapter, or which would prove useful for further understanding of the subject discussed in the chapter. Indeed a less intensive reading of collateral material might be preferable to an intensive reading of our chosen chapter alone. If you lay hands on the collateral reading do at least read one or two of the articles or relevant sections in full. Let us consider strategies for reading the textbook.

Reading the Textbook

A student at the tertiary level of education must discover a method which would enable him to feel at ease in the world of books. This confidence will be acquired and maintained by applying certain techniques which would help the student to gather the meaning of the book with speed and efficiency. This section on 'Reading' should help you in reconsidering the method you have been adopting over the years and, generally, in making you want to read your textbook.

The Title Page

It is one of those instructions I have been giving in this handbook which sounds ridiculous. But it is not. Some of us just glance at a title page and may not recall the accurate title when asked to do so. It is important to remember the exact word order in the title of a textbook and to write it down. This practice is important for the following reasons:

1. For future reference.
2. Another, perhaps even more important reason, is that the title would give a clue to the whole textbook, e.g. Christine Oppong's *Female and Male in West Africa.*
3. Apart from the general subject area with which a book concerns it self (e.g. literature) the book may also identify the specific emphasis which the book lends (e.g. Drama).
4. Read the title carefully also in order to find out the exact thing which the book discovers. For example, Alan P. Merriam's *The Anthropology of Music* which attempts to fuse cultural anthropology and ethnomusicology.
5. The sub-title must be given equal attention; read it very carefully. Sometimes the sub-title throws more light on the main title by pointing to the exact scope covered or manner in which a subject has been handled. The sub-title is separated from the main title by a colon (:) or a dash (–). Let us consider the following:

    (a) *Ngambika: Studies of Women in African Literature;* or
    (b) *Asemka: A Literary Journal of the University of Cape Coast.*

In these two examples the sub-titles are seen to play extremely important roles. The main titles are: Tshiluba and Akan words, respectively; while the sub-titles amplify the main titles and reach a much wider audience by using a language which is usually shared by a very large audience.

Let us look at this title: *Let the Trumpet Sound: The Life of Martin Luther King Jr.* by Stephen B. Oates. In this example, although the main title is expressed in the same language as the main title, the sub-title has given us the exact subject and scope. These three examples have been given to show that the sub-title is very important and must not be ignored.

Author's Name

After the title, note the correct name of the author. Again for the purposes of referencing and for proper documentation it is important to note the correct name of the author. If he is called Stephen make sure you do not write Steven. If she spells her first name Ama make sure you do not call her Amma. Apart from the name, note the credentials of the writer. Now this is important. For example, is the writer knowledgeable about the subject he/she is handling? A book on surgery written by a professor of surgery at a medical school will be worthy of the attention of a medical student. You need a source you can rely on when you are reading in order to gather information which will help you shape your own opinion on a subject.

Note the publishers of the textbook. University Presses can be trusted in the sense that they tend to have specialists as editors and they would usually scrutinize a manuscript and recommend it for publication only when they are satisfied that it meets the standards set for themselves. Other private, reputable publishers like Heinemann, George Allen and Unwin, Routeledge and Kegan Paul, just to name a few, have acquired for themselves the reputation of accepting very good manuscripts. Indeed your tutor will send you to a trusted source and when you note the publishers, it will help you in your own selection of additional reading material.

The date of publication is very important in determining how recent the material included in the book is. Usually, books take much, much longer to be published than do journals, for example; for this reason a book published in 1990 may have been written in 1985 whereas a journal published in 1990 may have included in it articles which were written only in 1988. Certainly there will be outdated but extremely important published texts in your discipline. Your tutor would guide you in your selection; try the personnel at your library; some of them can be very helpful in the selection of a current material in your discipline.

However, if you are reading 'psychology' it is not very useful to pick up a text book written thirty years ago when so much has been discovered and written on the subject since then. Certainly, if it was an essay written by Sigmund Freud or Carl Jung or some other giant in Psychology then it does not really matter how outdated the material is. You will discover in your reading even of the most recent material on the 'subconscious' that writers keep referring to S. Freud; in which case do not be put off from reading the original article by Freud because it is outdated.

Reading the Table of Contents

The table of contents is the key to the text: it provides a plan for the whole book. It provides the organization of the book and helps you to understand the sections into which the book is divided – it will indicate areas with which the book is concerned. As in our survey on reading the preface it is clear that few readers ever bother to read the table of contents. Most find it useful only in locating the exact chapter they are supposed to read. It is a good practice to read the table of contents before you get too busy with the details with which the chapter is concerned.

Read the table of contents for the following reasons:

1. To discover the outline of the textbook; pay attention to major divisions.
2. Each entry in the table of contents will speak to an aspect of the main topic handled in the textbook.
3. Find out how many chapters exist on the subdivision which your tutor has recommended for reading. You may consider the others as collateral reading material.

Let us consider the table of contents of *Female and Male in West Africa* edited by Christine Oppong and published by George Allen and Unwin in 1983.

Contents

Preface	
Acknowledgement	page xiii
List of Contributors	xvii
Map	xx

Statistical Framework
Part One: Overviews: Comparative Perspectives   3

Introduction to Part One   4

1.	Female and Male Life-Cycles by Helen Ware	6
2.	Female and Male Work Profiles by E.R. Fapohunda	32
3.	Patterns of Migration by Sex by A. Adepoju	54
	Conclusion to Part One	67

Case Studies — 69

Part Two: Male and Female Spheres: Separate and Connected — 71

	Introduction to Part Two	72
4.	Artistic and Sex Roles in a Limba Chiefdom by Simon Ottenberg	76
5.	The Political and Military Roles of Akan Women by Kwame Arhin	91
6.	The Feminine Sphere in the Institution of the Songhay-Zarma by Jeanne Bisiliat	99
7.	Dependence and Autonomy: the Economic Activities of secluded Hausa Women in Kano by Enid Schildkrout	107
8.	Marital Sexuality and Birth-Spacing among the Yoruba by Lawrence A. Adeokun	127
	Conclusion to Part Two	138

Part Three: Rights, Exchanges and Bargains: Cooperation and Conflict — 139

	Introduction to Part Three	140
9.	Who is a Wife? Legal Expression of Heterosexual Conflicts in Ghana by D.D. Vellenga	144
10.	The Separateness of Spouses: Conjugal Resources in an Ashanti Town by Katharine Abu	156
11.	Kinship and Cocoa Farming in Ghana by Christine Okali	169
12.	Fishmongers, Big Dealers and Fishermen: Co-operation and Conflict between the Sexes in Ghanaian Canoe Fishing by E. Vercruijsse	179
13.	Marriage, Divorce and Polygyny in Winneba by George Panyin Hagan	129
	Conclusion to Part Three	204

Part Four: Resources and Opportunities: Male Bias? — 207

	Introduction to Part Four	208
14.	Sex Roles in Nigerian Politics by K. Okonjo	211
15.	Skill-Building or Unskilled Labour for Female Youth: a Bauchi Case by C. Martin	223
16.	Conjugal Decision-Making: Some Data from Lagos by Wambui Wa Karanja	236
17.	Male Chauvinism: Men and Women in Ghanaian Highlife Songs by Nimrod Asante-Darko and Sjaak van der Geest	242
18.	Male and Female Factory Workers in Ibadan by Catherine M. di Demenico	256
19.	Female and Make Factory Workers in Accra by Eugenia Date-Bah	266
20.	Urban Contacts: a Comparison of Women and Men by Margaret Peil	275
	Conclusion to Part Four	283

Part Five: Individualism, Autonomy and Dependence: Migrants and Urban Dwellers — 285
Introduction to Part Five — 286

21.	Houses of Women: a Focus on Alternative Lifestyles in Katsina City by R. Pittin	291
22.	Gender Relations and conjugality among the Baule by Mona Etienne	303
23.	Avatime Women and Men, 1900-80 by L. Brydon	320
24.	Female and Male Domestic Cycles in Urban Africa: the Adabraka Case by Roger Sanjek	330
25.	Sugar Daddies and Gold-Diggers: the White Collar Single Women in Accra by C. Dinan	334
	Conclusion to Part Five	367

Postscript	370
References	374
Index	393

The table of contents reveals a five-part book for twenty-five essays written by twenty-five contributors, (read the credentials of the contributors). Each part has a clear heading which should lead you into the kinds of essays you are likely to find in them. Another observable feature of this table of contents is that each part has its own introduction and conclusion.The introductions are well written and they give you a brief summary of the actual contents of the essays. Perhaps you do not have to read the entire four-hundred page textbook to discover what it contains. These introductions to various sections of the textbook are very useful and they save on the time you would spend on reading.

Let us read the introduction to part one:

"This first part of the volume gives the regional framework for the subsequent detailed case studies, including fertility, mortality and migration, and for the educational and economic activities of the populations of the several countries of West Africa, showing the similarities and differences in economic and demographic behaviour of females and males.

Chapter 1 examines the divergent lives of men and women in West Africa as revealed by official statistics. From birth to death, the life chances and experiences of males and females are seen to be very different. Although the figures cannot convey the full flavour of everyday experience, they provide a guide to the scope and extent of the differences revealed later by sociologists and anthropologists. It is within this framework that Helen Ware examines sex differences in births. infant mortality, educational experience, marriage, fertility, and mortality. Inevitably, the emphasis is upon those countries for which adequate data are available: Senegal, Ivory Coast, Liberia, Ghana and Nigeria. However, the range of areas covered is sufficient to indicate those sex difference which are largely independent of culture (at least within West Africa) and those which are not. An examination of women's experiences as mothers, child-bearers and child-rearers is central; both in showing the biological experience of women, and in revealing the extent to which these alleged constraints fail to shape women's destinies. A salient fact emphasized, as in several of the later case studies, is that women of the region are both highly prolific – mothers of many children – and at the same time heavily engaged in productive work both inside and outside the home.

The second chapter, by Eleanor Fapohunda, examines work profiles of women and men in the region, again using available statistical source, which tend to give the impression that women are less economically active than men and that the extent of female involvement in the labour force over the life cycle varies between the West African countries and within them.

The chapter develops the theme of the similarity of male work experience and the dissimilarity of the female work patterns by looking at crude labour force participation rates, as well as by tracing the labour force participation rate patterns of the sexes in different countries. To illustrate the degree of dissimilarity of female work experience the case of Nigeria is examined in some detail; the country which supplies 52 per cent of West Africa's economically active female population. Within this context the female labour force participation patterns of several contrasting urban areas are compared and the shortcomings of the available statistics indicated.

The diverse female labour force participation patterns among and within West African countries are seen to reflect both the differing desire of women to seek employment outside the home and the extent of women's employment opportunities – themes which are taken up later in several case studies.

The concluding section of the chapter compares the occupational distribution of the sexes, noting that women tend to be concentrated in a more limited number of occupations than men, especially in the modern sector, in which men hold significantly more of the highly paid, high status jobs. Some of the factors causing the emergence of 'women's' occupations, as well as the implications in terms of income distribution status etc, are mentioned.

In chapter 3 Aderanti Adepoju examines the major trends in migration patterns among males and females in countries of West Africa that have pertinent data. In doing so he explores the determinants of the migration patterns in the different countries and cultural and ecological settings. The diverse opportunity structures facing males and females are discussed within the context of the developmental framework and the constraints imposed upon women by marriage and kin ties. In addition, so far as the data permit, recent changes in educational and employment opportunities are related to the apparent patterns of internal and international migration".

This introduction gives you an overview of what the section contains. You may proceed to read the various chapters according to your needs. The point is that you do not have to read the chapter till the middle only to discover that it does not respond to your needs. Remember what we said about the introduction and conclusion of individual chapters? You may apply them here as well. The introduction to the various essays will give you more information than the general introduction and the content will help you to decide if you should read the entire essay or not.

The table of contents of Christine Oppong's book also has a distinctive feature – conclusions to the various parts. Here a connecting thread to the various essays included in the section is drawn and the essence of the section is summed up. Let us look at the conclusion to part one.

"In this section we have given a comparative statistical framework for the case studies to follow. Certain important themes have been emphasized, such as the high levels of fertility and thus the high burden of child dependency borne by the parental generation, in populations half or more of which may be composed of children, and the associated physical consequences for women in terms of repeated pregnancy and lactation. At the same time women and men are heavily involved in agriculture, in the production and marketing food. Meanwhile, increasing numbers are migrating townward to seek urban sector employment. Women are noted to be more locally mobile than men, since many leave their natal homes at marriage, but over long distances and across national boundaries men have tended to migrate more. Migration trends are noted to be related to changing access to opportunities for employment and income generation. Thus, for instance, at the present time Ghana, which was formerly a country of heavy in-migration, is now undergoing a period of extensive out-migration.

This overall pattern of variables, including education, has been depicted to form the backcloth for the series of detailed micro studies to follow. The first set of such cases focuses upon the ways in which the life-spheres of women and men tend to be simultaneously separate and yet interconnected and complementary".

Reading the table of contents is a useful practice in preparing your mind for the actual details of the book.

Reading the Preface

A study of seventy students enrolled in an undergraduate course revealed that less than five per cent of the respondents ever read the preface to a text textbook. Some of the reasons advanced by the 95 per cent who did not included:

"irrelevant"	35%"
"never been asked to"	10%"
"never bothered"	55%

The preface to a book is important because in this section the readers hear the author speak. Here the author explains why he wrote the book in the first place, this reason may include the desire to respond to an identified need as in writing a book to help students acquire good study habits and writing skills which would help them perform better in school. Another reason may be writing a book to provide an alternative to the way a problem has been perceived over the years or to correct an assumption. There are perhaps as many reasons for writing as the books themselves.

The preface allows the author to say the following, among others:

1. His main reasons for writing the book.
2. The idea he wishes to convey in the book – or the central emphasis of the book.
3. The kinds of obstacles he came across.
4. His perception of the shortcomings of the book, and his apologies for them.

5. His attitude towards the premise which he has adopted in writing the book.
6. What the reader should gain from the book
7. The general structure of the book.
8. The experiences and qualifications of the author for undertaking to write the book.
9. The kind of audience he had in mind when writing the book i.e. whom the book is intended to serve.
10. Acknowledgement of indebtedness to those who funded, helped revise the text or assisted in the preparation of the book.

Can you identify any of these features in this preface taken from *African Women South of the Sahara* edited by Margaret Jean Hay and Sharon Stitcher and published by Longman in London in 1987?

"Academic interest in the study of women in Africa has grown enormously in the last few years. At the same time, among policy-makers, there has been a growing recognition of the importance of women's past and present contribution to African development. A large body of scholarly literature on African women has emerged, and university courses in African history, society and development and in black studies and women's studies, are beginning to incorporate material on African women.

It has been a challenge, however, to make the fruits of this new scholarship easily available to undergraduates and to the general reader. Much of the best work on African women is scattered in journals which are difficult to obtain or is still unpublished. In addition, most of it consists of detailed and specific case studies, which make the task of generalization somewhat daunting. There has long been a need for a general work on sub-Saharan African women, which would give an overview of the subject, would incorporate and synthesize the best insights of the new scholarship, and would at the same time be accessible to undergraduate readers.

We hope that the present volume will meet this need. It is an introductory, interdisciplinary text, written from the perspective of a number of disciplines but set by a specialist familiar with the issues in that particular field. Each introduces a topic in clear and straightforward terms, and attempts to point the way towards deeper study of the area discussed.

A note on our definition of the subject matter is in order. While focusing on the present, most of the chapters in this book also present a picture of African women in pre-colonial society, along with a consideration of the major changes occurring during the colonial era. Further, the information on women in South Africa has been integrated into the thematic discussion. We have not, however, included materials on women in Africa north of the Sahara, since the body of relevant scholarly literature is, unfortunately, still quite distinct from the materials and issues explored here.

The work reflects a combination of group effort and individual expertise. We think that the combination was a fruitful one. Although each chapter remains the individual creation of its author, each was written within editorial guidelines which attempted to ensure continuity and comprehensiveness. The prior circulation of outlines and drafts among contributors facilitated discussion and interchange, and in the end, contributed greatly to the book's internal cohesion.

Editorially, the work has been a joint effort in the fullest sense, both of us having worked together on all phases of the project. As editors, we would like to thank all the contributors for their hard work, patience, and good-humored willingness to accommodate revision. Iris Berger, Nancy Hafkin, and Chrisstraud Geary also deserve thanks for their assistance with particular aspect of this project. And finally, our appreciation goes to our editor, Peter Warwick, for his wise editorial advice and enthusiastic support for the project".

You may now pick up any of your textbooks and read the preface.

Reading the Index

The suggestion here is not to read the entire index: the purpose of the index is to make you aware of how the topics discussed in the book have been further broken down and under what chapters they may appear. The index is thus a useful guide to the contents of the book. If you need to assemble information which leads to a particular topic as it has been handled in the book, then the index will be of great help. You need to find out the possible classification under which a topic may be located.

The index can also be very useful when you want to test your level of comprehension. Let us consider this suggestion.

(a) Pick up any book with an index.
(b) Read the first fifty pages after you have followed the first three steps (of reading the book, the chapter, the paragraph).
(c) Turn to the index.
(d) Make a small vertical dash against all pages with references under 50, if you own the book.
(e) Try to remember what has been said about each entry.

If in doubt turn to the page. If you are able to remember it without referring to the page, cross the dash horizontally to achieve a cross.

The extent to which you can remember and retain the materials you have read should be quite obvious to you.

Let us emphasize a point we have been making all along – that you need to practice *constantly*. You have to apply what you have been reading to your textbooks and acquire the skill of reading with proficiency. After reading any material we have to rely on more than our memories to recall the contents of the reading material. Let us now consider some techniques for making notes.

Chapter 2

NOTE-MAKING AND NOTE-TAKING

In the chapter called READING we discussed the importance of reading your textbook in such a way as to extract the maximum information out of the activity. In this chapter we are going to consider ways of keeping on record what we read from our books and the substance of what we hear during lectures. These two activities, we should know by now, ought not be approached haphazardly if we mean to make the business of learning as pleasurable as it should be.

When we write notes or make them, what we should be doing is to keep a written record of the information we have either read or heard. If this is true then we ought to read and listen to our lectures with concentration. This point has already been emphasized in the previous chapter but you have not heard the end of it yet! Maybe when the student of mathematics is trying to work out her problems and the one in chemistry is figuring out equations in his area of study these two students may not have the same trouble trying to concentrate as the student of literature reading a novel, or another student trying to read a chapter in a history or psychology book, or listening to a lecture on the theories of social change. This is not to suggest that one subject is easier than the other; what we mean is that different doses of effort are required to work in various disciplines and at different activities, and that each student is required to pay attention to the activity of reading or listening.

The whole idea behind taking notes is to select and organize material from the reading and the lectures in such a way that we will remember them as accurately as possible. The lectures you will be attending will provide a huge percentage of the basis of your instruction at this level, irrespective of the size of the class or the lecturer's method of instruction. Certainly, subjects like mathematics or foreign languages may not be as suited to lecture-type presentation as others like economics, political science or geography. But however frequently or rarely used, the lectures which you attend should be recorded for future recall.

As a way of preparing to take notes you might want to avoid a notebook and start with loose sheets, because it is easier to add on to what you already have when you use loose sheets. For note-making as well as note-taking, you have to learn to be very liberal with paper.

Taking Notes from Lectures

When you have to attend your first lecture you may naturally have some apprehension about what it is all about. What you may probably perceive is that learning at this level is going to be different from what you experienced at the second-cycle level. You may have questions as to how much to write and how to go about it. Whatever you do, never attempt to write down everything you hear. This section proposes to address some of these concerns. Taking notes from lectures should be done in a systematic way; two main methods present themselves for our consideration: the outline and the summary.

The Outline

The outline form may be achieved by using sentences or phrases, headings or sub-heading to represent the content of the lecture. This method works best if the lecture itself is sufficiently well organized for the student to follow it logically. Let me tell you right away that this method will work best when you see a notice about a faculty lecture or an inter-faulty one in which a lecturer is going to share with the audience something he has come up with in his research; here a great effort has been brought to bear on the format of the lecture. But in our ordinary lectures to students what some of us normally do is to string the ideas we want to cover in the entire course in the form of an outline,˙ on which we extemporize. In the ordinary lecture room situation it is going to be difficult for you to instantly recognize in a very logical fashion the main points, their illustrations, the sub-points and their supporting material and write them all out neatly in the course of an hour or two. What you would want to do is to listen carefully and write done the main ideas of the lecture.

The Summary

Therefore, the summary and not the outline will be useful for taking notes during lectures. However, do not attempt to write down everything; it is unwise to make a literal shorthand transcription of the lecture even when you have the adequate skills. This brings us back to one basic question; how much should the student write? Here is the simple answer to the simple question - listen very carefully and write down only the gist of that lecture. What do we mean? Here we refer to the main points and inference of the lecture. You will surely miss these points and inferences if you do not listen with good concentration. You have to leave out illustrative anecdotes including the humorous jokes and the dry ones. If you listen very carefully to a lecture in your class you will notice that lecturers repeat themselves a lot, either by saying the same thing more than once or by finding more than one way of stating the same idea. Therefore, even when they are speaking very slowly and behaving as though they expect you to write down every word they do not intend that you should!

Usually, when defining the terminology of the discipline or stating the basic principles of an idea, they draw your attention to it and advise that you take down word for word those definitions and rules; in your reading from books later on you will have occasion to elaborate on them.

If you have difficulty hearing the lecturer's voice or if you do not understand something never hesitate to raise your hand and politely make your point; the same goes with your disagreement over an issue. Remember you may be asking a question which is of interest to other members of the class, and you will be creating the situation where the lecturer will have to find another way of stating the issue. Questions are always useful in helping us evaluate both the content and the form of lectures. Teachers never expect their students to be passive in the learning process; they want your minds to be continually agitated and they appreciate it when students demonstrate that they are capable of independent thinking.

Later on, away from the lecture theatre you will have to look over the notes you took in order to make sure that what you have written down is intelligible to you. There are times when you will resort to all manner of abbreviations, semi-shorthand and various ways of representing the words that you use very often. Just make sure that you can make meaning out of all those beautiful designs and patterns when you return to them.

Making Notes from Reading

In chapter one, we considered some of the ways of reducing the paragraph into a sentence or two, as a way of keeping a record of the substance of our reading. You will do well to remind yourself of that procedure of summarization as one way of making notes. When we have revised our rough and often hasty summaries into close and precise ones which provide a faithful reflection of the content of our reading, and when such writing shows that we have paid attention to style and form then we have moved from a simple summary into a precis. The precis is very useful to the secretarial student because later on he will have to capture the gist of reports, articles, speeches or letters for a boss who will not have the time to read the entire document. The precis should stay close to the original content and style of the author, unless the author is verbose or repetitive in style.

Another way of making notes from your reading is to make an outline which represents the gist of your reading in a graphic form. As we stated under "Taking notes from lectures" the outline form is more appropriate to taking or making notes when the material itself is so presented that it is easy to grasp the skeleton of thought. The textbooks in your area of study would have been well constructed to allow you to find out the thread of progression in any given discussion. You may proceed in a way like this:

1. main idea

    a. supporting idea

        i. other illustration

One way of going about the outline is to divide your page into three columns. On the right side write the main ideas of the passage, in the middle section write the supporting ideas, while the examples and minor ideas may be written in the third column.

Write an outline for the following passage:

Events taking shape in India and in China were to make a permanent imprint on the worldwide pattern of the drug trade. Arab traders had probably introduced opium in that part of the world around the 8th. century when they established commercial ties with merchants in the port of Canton; Chinese Literature first mentions the drug around this time. By the 16th. century, the use of opium was widespread in both India and in China, and the number of addicts was quite substantial.

The Chinese were quick to recognize the gravity of their opium addiction problem, and as early as 1729 the sale of opium for smoking and the keeping of opium dens were banned by the emperor. But the prohibitions had little effect, and as the vast Chinese market continued to expand, India became its chief supplier.

Warren Hastings, appointed the first Governor-General of India in 1773, established a system of selling opium concessions to generate government revenue. Around 1857, more that 100,000 acres were under opium cultivation in the plains of Central India and in the alluvial valley of the Ganges, land that had formerly been used for the cultivation of sugar, indigo, wheat and other grains.

Finally the Chinese took determined action. Lin Ze-Xu, a strict Confucian, was sent to Canton by the emperor as a special commissioner to eradicate the opium trade once and for all. Within two months of his arrival in the spring of 1839, he had made 1,600 arrests and confiscated and destroyed 11,000 pounds of opium. But the unforgivable act – as far as the British were concerned – came when Li ordered that Canton be completely closed to all foreign trade.

Britain declared war and within three years soundly defeated the Chinese. China was required to cede the island of Hong Kong, allow free trade in her ports and to pay a heavy indemnity of twenty-one million dollars to compensate Britain for the opium that had been destroyed and the cost of conducting the war.

The opium trade flourished. The British colonial government of Hong Kong encouraged opium smugglers to operate out of its harbour, and the colony established itself as the world's key opium distribution centre.

Britain continued to pressure China into legalizing opium and did everything it could to frustrate Chinese enforcement efforts. Finally, an opium war broke out. The Chinese central government was too hamstrung by factionalism to offer much resistance, and the combined British and French forces advanced as far north as Peking, where they proceeded to loot the capital. The importation of opium was made legal, and a fixed price for the drug was set.

The Chinese emperor had requested that a heavy duty be placed on opium, but of course this had been quite unacceptable to the British. By 1880, the addict population was believed to be in excess of 15 million.

The pattern of the opium trade had been set by a rapacious Western trade policy, particularly that of Britain, whose officials remained unmoved by the tragic spectacle of 15 million addicts in a proud nation almost crushed by its own shame. But in a strange and ironic twist of history the West would become the victim of its own success in this venture.

Andre Mcnicoll: *Drug-Trafficking: A North South Perspective*

Can you try to make notes on this passage first by reading it over once more and then writing a sentence to sum up each paragraph as we tried to do under the chapter titled 'Reading'? You may certainly read over that chapter in order to refresh your memory about the topic word and how it functions in the sentence. After the exercise you may have something like these sentences.

The introduction of opium by Arab traders led to the addiction of Indians and Chinese.

The ban on the smoking of opium had very little effect on the Chinese.

Opium was cultivated to generate British government revenue.

The British declared war on China when Canton was closed to foreign trade.

Defeated, China was forced to give up Hong Kong, allow free trade and pay Britain for the cost of the war.

Hong Kong became the world's key opium distribution centre.

The opium trade was finally legalized.

The British rejected the Chinese request of a heavy duty on the commodity.

The West now pays a terrible price for the use of opium by its own people.

You may make notes out of this passage in three main ways:

1. Write a summary of these points in one paragraph which you may later on edit make a precis.
2. You may also write an outline of the passage by using the format which goes with the letters a, b, c, etc.
3. It is also possible to make notes by dividing your page into three and arranging the main ideas, the supporting ideas and the minor illustrations accordingly.

You are expected to do all these three exercises! So please get on with them.

Chapter 3

BASIC SENTENCE PATTERNS

Although there are no rules about the length of sentences that you may write at this stage, there are a few guidelines about what a sentence should look like. Every sentence should have at least two parts: (a) a SUBJECT and (b) a VERB. These two parts form the basis of every sentence and are sometimes called the immediate constituents of the sentence. The subject refers to the object, idea, thing or person who is of basic concern in the sentence. The verb refers to what the subject does. Therefore, it is quite possible to have a complete, grammatically correct sentence with just two words as in the following.

Gases react.

Language changes.

Plants photosynthesize.

Birds fly.

Religion comforts.

Food satisfies.

Refrigerators preserve.

AIDS destroys.

Debts accrue.

Can you think of two sentences in your subject area which are patterned after the Subject-Verb format as in the examples shown? Do write such sentences down in the space provided below:

a. ....

....

b. ....

....

Some sentences will require at least one more part, AN OBJECT, in order to make the sense complete. The OBJECT tells us that the verb needs something else to complete its meaning. Examples:

Acids attack metals.

Oxygen oxidizes iron.

Jesus demonstrated humility.

Farmers produce crops.

Teachers transmit ideas.

Students develop skills.

Carnivores eat flesh.

Demand determines prices.

Cleanliness saves lives.

In the space provided below try to compose two sentences which would correspond to the subject you are studying:

a. ....

b. ....

....

Subject-Verb Complement

Subject-Verb Complement: The complement throws more light on the nature of the subject as in the following examples:

Bombs are dangerous.

Men are mammals.

Adam Smith was an economist.

They became University students.

Yaa Asantewaa was described as a patriot.

The child is happy.

Do provide below two examples of sentences constructed in the Subject-Verb-Complement mode; remember to reflect your courses in your sentences.

a. ....

....

b. ....

....

Subject-Verb-Object-Complement

Subject-Verb-Object-Complement: In this sentence type the complement gives some more information about the object as in the following examples:

    He named the substance alcohol.

    Haemoglobin makes blood red.

    Kwame Nkrumah was elected President.

    The manager appointed her as farm overseer.

    Italy made Sicily her colony.

    Culture makes man a human being.

Homer wrote THE ILIAD, a book of poetry

In the space below provide two sentences after the Subject-Verb-Object-Complement pattern to reflect the kind of courses you are pursuing at this stage:

a. ....

....

b. ....

....

Subject-Verb-Object-Adverb

In this sentence type the new word is the adverb which is a little word that can be broken down further into two little words - ad and verb in order to help us to understand its function. The adverb throws more light on the state of the verb.

Here are some examples:

    Accountants manipulate accounts wisely.

    Sports bring people together.

    Auguste Comte used the term "sociology" first.

    Development helps society enormously.

    She visited her daughter at dawn.

    The farmer harvested the crops in January.

    He mixed the substances quickly.

Your two examples:

a. ....

....

b. ....

....

Subject-Verb-Object-Object

This is the kind of sentence which requires another object in order to make the sense complete. Examples of this sentence type are found in the following:

    Leaves manufacture food for plants.

    Education offers us knowledge.

The agricultural officer gave the farmers some insecticides.

Biology is the study of plants and animals.

Fuel costs us money.

The student showed the counselor her essay.

Your two examples:

a. ....

....

b. ....

....

Now, a word of caution: although we said in the first sentence type that in order for any sentence to be complete it must have at least a subject and a verb, it is necessary to add that whatever the shape of the sentence, it must make sense. This is what we mean – a sentence like the following,

> The mango swallowed the house

is a grammatically correct sentence although it makes no sense at all. Sometimes some long sentences do not make sense because the writer gets lost in his or her thoughts and in the process may leave behind an important component of the sentence and produce a long but incomplete sentence like this one:

> The general view about physical exercises is that the use of gross muscle groups to generate heat and energy in the body for a person's total strength, health and recreation.

This sentence is incomplete because it has no main verb and no predicate. Sometimes even short sentences which have the desired grammatical items can also be incomplete. Let us look at these two sentences:

> Because he slept late.
> The reason why he is not here.

Both sentences are grammatically correct but their meaning is not clear. In this case we may try and join the sentences to form one sentence as in the following:

The reason why he is not here is that he slept late.

The expansion of the basic sentence may be done through two main ways: coordination and subordination.

Introduction
Coordination and Subordination are means of connecting ideas. In order to convey your thoughts effectively in writing, it is important to arrange these thoughts in such a way that you coordinate the ideas you wish to give equal importance to, as in the ideas about good grades in this sentence:

I expect to make good grades and I am working very hard at my courses.

The clause beginning with *because* is subordinate to the main clause because it plays a minor role in the entire statement. Information which is subordinated may be very important to the total meaning of the whole sentence but it plays a less important role to the subject and predicate of the main clause of the sentence.

Words, phrases, clauses and sentences may be connected by using the coordinating conjunctions **and, but, or, nor, for, so,** and the pairs (sometimes called correlative conjunctions) **either-or, neither-nor**. Other words which sometimes function as coordinating conjunctions to connect words, phrases, clauses and sentences include **yet, only while.**

When joining independent clauses, conjunctive adverbs act like coordinating conjunctions – **so, however, consequently, hence, moreover, furthermore, also, accordingly likewise, anyhow, besides, indeed, thus, meanwhile, namely, and then** – although it should be borne in mind that as their names indicate, they also have an adverbial function.

You may subordinate ideas or facts by expressing them in clauses introduced by subordinating conjunctions such as **after, although, because, as if, as, when, where, while,** or by relative pronouns such as **who, which, that.** A number of subordinating conjunctions are phrases several words long: **as a result, for that matter,** etc.

Coordination

Relating Equal Ideas through Coordination
The kinds of relationship between coordinate clauses are:

addition

> contrast
> choice
> result

Addition

The following connectives are used to indicate that although both statements are of equal rank, what follows the connective is supplementary to what precedes it.

Example: I love him and he loves me.

> also
> and
> besides
> both
> furthermore
> likewise
> moreover
> then

Contrast

The following connectives are used to introduce an idea which, although of equal rank, stands in conflict or contrast to what precedes.

Example: I love him but he does not love me.

> but
> however
> nevertheless
> still
> yet

Choice

The following connectives are used to suggest an alternate possibility.

Example: I love him or you love him.

> either ... or
> neither ... nor
> or
> otherwise

Result
The following connectives are used to state the consequence or result of a preceding statement.

Example: I love him therefore he loves me.

>accordingly
>consequently
>hence
>therefore

You will have to develop the technique of detecting the relation which exists between sentences that appear to have equal importance. This is an area where the use of coordinating conjunctions gains significance. Compare the following passages:

>The University of Cape Coast has five faculties. Each faculty offers both undergraduate and graduate programmes. The student population is just under two thousand. This is a very small number. The actual capacity of the University is about three times higher. The lecture theaters are not fully utilized. Also, the new halls of residence are progressing at a very slow rate. The existing library is a sorry apology for an academic institution.

>The University of Cape Coast has five faculties which offer both undergraduate and graduate programs, yet the student population is very small. As a result, the lecture theaters are not fully utilized. Some of the factors which account for the low levels of enrollment include inadequate sources of funding, outdated equipment and lack of accommodation.

The details in both passages are essentially the same, but the second passage is easier to follow. Don't you think so? Whereas the first passage has a string of sentences together without relating them, the second passage relates coordinate points about the problem of a low population at the University of Cape Coast with the reasons which account for this problem.

Faulty Coordination

Before any two or more statements can be coordinated correctly it is important to establish a relationship between them. Statements which have no sensible connection between them or those which appear to contradict common sense may lead to faulty coordination. There are other times when a faulty coordination occurs because the writer has been careless in leaving out important information. Let us consider these examples:

Faulty   Ekua took a long vacation, and her health did not improve.
Revised   Ekua took a long vacation, but her health did not improve.

Contrast
Faulty   Ekua spent a long time in the hospital, but she came out entirely well.

Revised   Ekua spent a long time in the hospital; consequently she came out entirely well.

Result
Did you notice the difference in punctuation with the commas and the semi-colon? I believe you did and so I want to explain: when used to coordinate clauses, the conjunctions **and, or, nor, yet and but are** usually preceded by a comma, while the semi-colon precedes conjunctions like accordingly, consequently, nevertheless, moreover, likewise, therefore, otherwise, however, furthermore. (Chapter Nine deals with punctuation in detail). Excessive use of the coordination can lead to statements with unclear thoughts.

Exercises on Coordination

In the space provided express each of the following strings of sentences in one sentence by inserting a coordinating conjunction:

Example:
> I apologized to her. She will not forgive me.
> I apologized to her but she will not forgive me.

1. We planned on waking up late that day. We were very upset by the noise from the village.

   ....

   ....

   ....

Basic Sentence Patterns 39

2. They read the revised rules for the halls of residence. They disagreed with all the major changes.

   ....
   ....
   ....

3. The footballer was hurt during the training session. He will not be able to play for a while.

   ....
   ....
   ....

4. Under these circumstances, your voice must be heard. No one will know of your actual role in this enterprise.

   ....
   ....
   ....

5. That hall magazine publishes some of the best essays by students. It is in financial ruins.

   ....
   ....
   ....

6. The Ghanaian economy has depended for too long on cocoa. Some people fear the economic consequences of the virus which is destroying cocoa pods.

   ....
   ....
   ....

7. There was interruption of electricity that day. We could not hold our evening classes.

   ....
   ....
   ....
   ....

8. The hall warden told us to take good care of university property. She said the hall council would make us pay for repairs.

   ....
   ....
   ....
   ....

9. The bad news about my mother's death was quite unexpected. It took me several years to recover from the shock.

   ....
   ....
   ....
   ....

10. He searched through her closet. He was surprised at finding no incriminating evidence.

    ....
    ....
    ....
    ....

11. I once had a cold. It gave me a terrible headache. I went to visit the doctor. He said I had a sinus infection.

   ....
   ....
   ....
   ....
   ....

12. That wing of Adehye Hall has some of the finest ladies I have ever met. They sweep the floors. They scrub the sinks. They keep the noise level low.

   ....
   ....
   ....
   ....
   ....

13. You want to make a phone call. You must go to the telephone exchange. You must have the call booked. You have to wait for a while. You have to shout your way through the conversation.

   ....
   ....
   ....
   ....
   ....

14. I had a terrible day. My son broke out in measles at dawn. I missed my class for the second time.

....

....

....

....

....

Subordination

When the arrangement of ideas or facts is such that they are not of equal rank, those on the lower rank are subordinate. The subordinate clause works to throw light on the main clause; the main clause can stand on its own, but the subordinate clause amplifies the main clause and so cannot stand on its own. We will illustrate by using one or two examples which will help to clarify matters about subordination:

> My sister, who is an efficient manager, designed a course on personal relations for her firm. The independent clause – *My sister designed a course on personal relations for her firm* – has greater emphasis than the other clause; it can also stand on its own. The clause – *who is an efficient manager* is subordinate to the main clause; it has lesser emphasis, it throws light on the main clause and it cannot stand on its own as an independent structure. Remember the components of a sentence?

Here is another example:

> Political kings who were once very powerful are now negligible. The independent clause – *The political Kings are now negligible* – is the main clause, has greater emphasis, while – *which at one time was very powerful* – has lesser emphasis; it is subordinate and it helps to modify the main clause.

Isolate the independent and subordinate clauses in the following sentences:

1. The student leader who was able to maintain the peace had a first class degree.

I   ....

    ....

S   ....

    ....

2. We felt so relieved when the rains finally stopped.

I   ....

    ....

S   ....

    ....

3. The report indicated that several people who smoke profusely are aware of the health hazards created by the habit.

I   ....

    ....

S   ....

    ....

4. The Chief Counsellor, convinced of the importance of the work, set up a committee chaired by the president of JCR.

I   ....

    ....

S   ....

    ....

5. Yaa Asantewaa, persuaded by a deep sense of justice, led the war against imperial domination.

I ....

....

S ....

....

The relationship which exists between the independent and subordinate clauses is usually made clear by the kind of subordinating conjunction which introduces the subordinate clause. Time, condition, result or purpose and reason or cause are some of the kinds of relationships which can exist between the subordinate adverbial clause and the independent clause. It is important to note that some of the conjunctions will appear under more than one heading because they can be used in more than one way.

Time
The relationship between the ideas expressed in the subordinate clause and the independent clause may be stated by introducing clauses which express a time relationship:

Example: You must not get up from the dinner table until you have finished eating all your vegetables.

Think up a sentence to express time relationship between an independent clause and a subordinate one by using the following subordinating conjunctions:

since

....

....

when

....

....

as

....

....

while

....

....

before

....

....

until

....

....

after

....

....

whenever

....

....

Condition
The subordinating conjunctions in this section introduce the state in which the independent clause gains validity:

Example: **Even though** his parents had expressed disapproval about the relationship, he continued to see the girl. (The clause typed in **both** letters explains the condition under which he continued to see the girl.)

Using each of the following subordinating conjunctions construct sentences you are likely to write in your essays:

provided

....

....

unless

....

....

if

....

....

while

....

....

Result or Purpose
Subordinating conjunctions are also used to express the result or purpose of an idea expressed in the independent clause.

Purpose: It is important to have a good laboratory, so that students can carry on the relevant experiments. (The subordinate clause – *so that students can carry on the relevant experiments* – states the purpose of a good laboratory as explained in the independent clause).

Result: People generally reasoned with their hearts and not their minds so that it became impossible to reach an objective conclusion.

Form two sentences each with the following subordinating conjunctions to express the result or purpose of the idea carried in the independent clause:

than

....

....

in order that

....

....

so that

....

....

as a result of

....

....

Reason or Cause
The subordinate clause in this category, introduced by the subordinating conjunctions, helps to explain why something occurred in the independent clause.

Example: We postponed the meeting because we did not form a quorum.

Construct a sentence with each of the following subordinating conjunctions to reflect the courses that you are taking:

since

....

....

because

....

....

as

....

....

whereas

....

....

Exercises on Subordination

In the following strings of sentences you will find one which has been typed in the bold style. Use that sentence as the main sentence pattern or independent clause and subordinate the other sentences to it. Write your sentence in the spaces provided after each string of sentences. Here is an example:

> **The student leader took his academic work very seriously.** He eventually made a four point average.

Because the student leader took his academic work seriously, he made a four point average.

1. It was burning hot. Our team lost the football match. **We wished we had gone to the beach instead.**

   ....

   ....

   ....

2. **I bought two files from the University Bookshop.** One was for my student. The other had to be returned.

   ....

   ....

   ....

Basic Sentence Patterns 49

3. He enjoyed his classes in biology. He enjoyed his classes in chemistry. **He enjoyed his liberal courses more than either of them.**

   ....
   ....
   ....
   ....

4. **Several students do not know what to do after graduating.** The Universities need guidance experts to help them out.

   ....
   ....
   ....
   ....

5. I just graded her latest paper. **She is capable of good work.** She needs to be motivated.

   ....
   ....
   ....
   ....

6. The jury heard the case of the rapist. It ordered a new trial. **The activists were greatly offended.**

   ....
   ....
   ....
   ....

7. He woke up suddenly. The hall of residence was very quiet. He saw two men dragging another towards the common room. **He was perplexed.**

8. The day was long. The boy missed his parents. He walked towards the playground. **He started painting graffiti on the school building.**

9. The messenger apologized for his sloppiness again. **The supervisors paid no attention.** They remembered the last time he rendered an apology for sloppiness.

10. **His leg had not properly healed.** He insisted on taking part in the game. His friends were upset by his decision.

   ....
   ....
   ....
   ....
   ....

11. The Central Committee will reach a decision today. There has been a great deal of argument. **The Students Representative Council will not support such a confrontational attitude.**

   ....
   ....
   ....
   ....
   ....

12. There are too many hawkers on this campus. The kiosks are unsightly. They leave the campus littered with garbage. **They pose a health hazard.**

   ....
   ....
   ....
   ....
   ....

13. The holidays are normally too short. The examination papers are too many. The meetings are too long and unproductive. **University teachers are really overburdened and terribly underpaid.**

   ....
   ....
   ....
   ....
   ....

14. **The role of a mother is very challenging.** She is normally the first to wake up and the last to go to bed. She plays roles that range from the clown to the medical doctor.

   ....
   ....
   ....
   ....
   ....

15. I have visited you four times. You have visited me once. Do I have to keep doing this? **I am having a hard time understanding this latest definition of love.**

   ....
   ....
   ....
   ....
   ....

Chapter 4

SUBJECT-VERB AGREEMENT

While constructing your sentences it is extremely important to establish the correct relationship between the subject and the verb. This simply means that if the subject is singular (one), the verb should also be in the singular form; a singular form of the verb must agree with a singular noun, as in these examples:

The African folktale is an important tool for the education and entertainment of the younger members of the community.

Cocoa contains such alkaloids like theobromine and caffeine.

A manager is a person who has been placed in a responsible position to supervise, direct and monitor the activities of his subordinates; he is accountable to his supervisors.

Dispersal of fruits by animals *is achieved* in a variety of ways.

In these examples the singular nouns have been underlined, while the corresponding singular forms of the verbs have been typed in italics. In the spaces created below compose two sentences of your own to show the agreement between a singular subject and a singular form of the verb. Make sure that the sentences will tell you and your reader something about what you are studying:

a.
....

....

....

b ....

....

....

Plural nouns (more than one) have to agree with the *plural* forms of the verbs. Let us take a look at these examples:

Plants which possess an enclosed seed convered by a seed coat and have testa are called flowering plants.

Some *fungi* cause disease in plants.

Fixed *assets* suffer physical deterioration through usage and the passage of time.

Non-residential students have halls of affiliation.

In most verbs the singular has an "s" while the plural does not. The placement of that "s" should be carefully noted because it has been the cause of a considerable number of grammatical errors in student writing. Let us illustrate with a couple of examples:

(a)   Acid corrodes

(b)   Acids corrode

In the first example, "acid" is singular and so the singular form of the verb is marked by the inflection "s"; whereas in the second, there is no "s" on the verb form because it agrees with a plural noun.
There are three instances in which this otherwise quite simple rule is modified; being aware of these modifications will help in eliminating some of the grammatical errors that students are wont to make. Read these instances and their illustrations very carefully.
When the singular subjects are defined by the words *each, every, anyone, everybody, nobody, somebody, no one,* the impression is immediately, and as a result, the singular form of the verb is employed.

Examples:
1. In this University each man and woman studies for good grades.

2. *Every* child and adult has to pay a fee in order to watch the film.

3. *Anyone* who *thinks* he has the answer can try out the puzzle.

4. *Everybody* is required to submit a medical certificate for consideration.

5. *Nobody has* the right to take another's life.

6. *Somebody has* taken a stand on this issue.

7. *No one dares* to disagree with the decision of the committee.

The singular form of the verb is used when the two singular nouns connected with the word "and" refer to the same subject or idea.

Examples:
1. My study-mate and president of the JCR *has* to make that decision.

2. Her sister and manager *works* hard for her firm.

3. Thorough reorganization and reinforcement takes time.

In the case of mathematical computation, as in that of the pronouns *any* and *none*, you are never likely to make a mistake because both the singular and plural forms of the verb may be employed.

Examples:
1. Six plus four *is* ten
   or
2. Six plus four *are* ten

3. *Is any* one of these good enough for you?

4. *Were any* of my students involved in the fund-raising exercise?

5. *None are* likely to fail such a test.

6. *None survives* better than this race of people.

It is generally agreed, however, that, although both forms are grammatically correct, in the case of *none* and *any*, the singular be used in a formal style, while the plural be employed in the informal.

In the case of collective nouns like *band, majority, crowd, faculty, jury, family, clergy, audience*, either the singular or the plural form of the verb may be used depending on whether the group is being considered as one unit or the members are being considered individually.

Examples:
The *jury* normally acts very swiftly in deciding such cases.
They *jury* were unable to reach a verdict after three days.

My *family* celebrates every birthday in a modest manner.
My *family* hold the most divergent views on the subject.

The *audience* applauds at the end of each performance.
The *audience* were divided in their appreciation of the play.

The *faculty* of the University of Cape Coast is an eminent one.
The *faculty* have voted against the new housing policy.

The *majority* of Ghanaians prefer constitutional rule.
The *majority* wants its side to be heard all the time.

An instance in which the singular form of the verb is required is when two or more singular subjects are connected by the words *but, neither, nor, either, or, but.*

Examples:
1.   Neither salt nor pepper is good for my health.

2.   Either the Sciences or the Arts is likely to admit her.

3.   Not only his roommate, but his girl friend finds him withdrawn.

Sometimes things are not so simple, as when one of the words connected by *or, but, nor* is singular and the other is plural; at times like these one can quite be at a loss as to which form of the verb is grammatically correct. There is a very simple answer to this problem - just look at the status of the subject closer to the verb and make that verb agree with it. In other words, if the noun closer to the verb is singular, you required the singular verb, and the reverse is true.

Examples:
Neither the doctor nor the *nurses were* available for comment.
Neither the nurses nor the *doctor was* available for comment

Either the leader or the *followers manage* the estate.
Either the followers or the *leader manages* the estate.

Not just the children but even the *parent has* no self-control.
Not just the parent but even the *children have* no self-control.

When a singular subject is followed immediately by such group of words like *as well as, in addition to, including, no less than, with, together with*, or any such similar construction, the singular verb is required no matter the status of the subject that comes after these words.

Examples:
1. The *student* as well as the lecturers has the credit for such high performance.
2. *My notebook* in addition to my files is missing.
3. Their *mother* no less than their father contributes towards their education.
4. The *Chief Executive* together with his assistant *was* elected into office.

In the event that such constructions prove either illogical or awkward, avoid them and re-write those sentences in such a way as to achieve clarity:

1. *Both* the student and the lecturers *have* the credit for such high performance.
2. My notebook *and* my files *are* missing.
3. Their *parents contribute* towards their education.
4. The Chief Executive *and* his assistant *were* elected into office.

When a singular subject is followed by a plural modifier, a singular verb is required.

Examples:
1. The *vision* of past directors *is* worthy of attention.
2. One of my children has a very good appetite.
3. A *brochure* which *contains* all the courses offered in the faculty helps students immensely.

In the case where the subject is a relative pronoun, the verb must agree with the antecedent of that pronoun.

Examples:
1. This is one of the scientists who *work* on the AIDS vaccine.
2. Here is an example of my paintings which *demonstrate* my philosophy.
3. She has been one of the women who *encourage* young girls.
4. His son is one of the boys who *play* tennis.

When a plural noun is used to indicate a sum or unit, the singular verb is required.

Examples:
1. *Fifty per cent* is the minimum required to pass this course.
2. *A hundred years* in the life of mankind is insignificant.
3. *One million pounds sterling* is a lot of money any time.
4. *Twenty minutes is* too long a time to wait in such a weather.
5. *Two kilometres is* a good distance to run everyday.

Some words exist in the plural form but are usually singular in meaning and as a result, these plural nouns take on the singular verb. Here we have in mind such words like *news, economics, mathematics, ethics, whereabouts, electronics, acoustics, athletics.*

1. The *whereabouts* of his son is still unknown to him.
2. The *news has* to be read every hour.
3. *Mathematics offers* her the most satisfaction.
4. The *ethics* of this sect is highly questionable.
5. *Semantics is* useful for those interested in linguistic development.

The words *it* and *there* may be used as anticipatory subjects – what this means is that the true subjects come later in the sentence. Used this way, these words are called expletives. However, *It* is always followed by a singular verb while **there** may take either the singular or plural form of the verb, depending on the nature of the subject.

Examples:
1. *There is no excuse* for forgetting her birthday.
2. *There are* several ways to kill a cat.
3. *It is* not clear what you mean by this statement.

Note that expletive constructions to do not have much steam; avoid excessive use of such weak forms.

Exercises on Subject-Verb Agreement

Instructions:

(a) Select the appropriate verb form from the options provided in the parenthesis.

Subject-Verb Agreement

(b) In the space provided after each exercise, explain how you arrived at your choice:

1. Either loose or periodic sentences (is/are) necessary in good writing; both are used by all writers.

   ....
   ....
   ....

2. The President of the SRC presented his views to the committees which (was/were) corrected and amended.

   ....
   ....
   ....

3. He seldom (laughs/laugh) and when he (does/do) it (seems/seem) so forced.

   ....
   ....
   ....

4. The use of standard English in all forms of writing (furthers/further) her chances of being successful.

   ....
   ....
   ....

5. One of the members of the family (was/were) elected as successor to the throne.

   ....
   ....
   ....

6. Having put my academic programme first, extracurricular activities (comes/come) as a close second.

   ....
   ....
   ....

7. The business letter and the technical report must be handled in minimum time; so both of these, especially the business letter, (tends/tend) to use short paragraphs.

   ....
   ....
   ....

8. Kwame, together with some of his friends, (is/are) in deep trouble with the disciplinary committee.

   ....
   ....
   ....

9. The secretary's only excuse (continues/continue) to be the many interruptions he has to put up with.

   ....
   ....
   ....

10. There (is/are) enough noise in the Hall without parties and dawn prayers.

    ....
    ....
    ....

Subject-Verb Agreement

11. Athletics in the revised curriculum (has/have) become both varied and extensive.

    ....
    ....
    ....

12. Neither the Vice-Chancellor nor faculty members (takes/take) such a decision.

    ....
    ....
    ....

13. There (is/are) too many grammatical errors in this essay.

    ....
    ....
    ....

14. The sprinter who (gets/get) to the crossroads first (has/have) a big advantage.

    ....
    ....
    ....

15. The good news (is/are) that she won that tough competition.

    ....
    ....
    ....

16. Twenty-five percent discount on that jacket (does/do) not appear to be a very good bargain.

   ....
   ....
   ....

17. Either Physics or Electronics (is/are) very useful for everyone in that discipline.

   ....
   ....
   ....

18. One of the disasters which often (occurs/occur) when you are traveling is to arrive at your destination without your luggage.

   ....
   ....
   ....

19. The member of parliament as well as the assemblyman (was/were) highly commended.

   ....
   ....
   ....

20. Either the uncle or the nephews (has/have) to attend this important meeting.

   ....
   ....
   ....

21. The clergy (makes/make) the big decisions on such matters.

   ....

   ....

   ....

22. There (is/are) highly confidential reports that always (manages/manage) to acquire publicity.

   ....

   ....

   ....

23. What the geologist is looking for (is/are) evidence of the history of the earth.

   ....

   ....

   ....

24. The drug dealer, together with his agents, (was/were) arrested outside the city.

   ....

   ....

   ....

25. After twenty-five exercises on the subject-verb agreement, banku and okro soup (is/are) the food to make up for your lost energy.

   ....

   ....

   ....

Chapter 5

AMBIGUITIES AND DANGLING MODIFIERS

Ambiguities

A sentence or part of a sentence is ambiguous when it conveys more than one meaning. There are times when an ambiguous sentence is intended by the writer, as when poets intentionally use words or constructions in such a way that multiple meanings can be inferred; puns are also deliberately ambiguous. However, our concern here lies with the ambiguous statement which is not intended; this is a feature of bad writing which usually results from a careless use of the sentence structure and a failure to include in the sentence the signals which will make the meaning clear. With this kind of writing the reader is obliged to read over the work a few times and make some effort to discover what the writer wants to say. There is no point putting your instructor through this kind of torture and reducing your chances of making a good grade.

The interesting thing about ambiguous sentences is that they are usually grammatically correct and on first reading they look quite safe from negative criticism, but they are not. Consider this sentence:

The train was long.

This sentence has a subject – the train, a verb – was, and a compliment – long. From the point of view of grammar, the sentence is correct, yet it is ambiguous because the lexical item – train – is ambiguous because it could either refer to the mode of transportation which moves along the railroad or the part which is attached to a bridal gown. This kind of ambiguity is lexical because one word in the sentence is the source of the confusion.

Ambiguities can occur when we cannot clearly identify the constituents of a sentence. Consider this sentence:

The guests who saw the hall durbar frequently highly commended it.

The problem with this sentence is that if you were asked to divide it into its immediate constituents, that is, the subject and the predicate, you will have a hard time deciding whether to place the cut before or after the word "frequently". Either of the following might be intended by the writer:

The guests who attended the hall durbar / frequently commended it.

The guests who attended the hall durbar frequently / commended it.

The difficulty which leads to the ambiguity is created by the placement of the adverb **frequently** between the verb clusters **saw the durbar** and **commended it** and the adverb could go both logically and grammatically with either verb cluster. In this respect the following are not ambiguous because the meaning is not open to more than one interpretation:

> The guests who frequently saw the hall durbar commended it.
> (frequently" in this position applies to the verb "saw").

> The guests who attended the hall durbar commended it frequently.
> (in this position, frequently applies to the verb "commended").

Ambiguity in Noun Clusters

Noun clusters offer various possibilities of ambiguity. Consider this statement:

> I saw the student in the bus that had been grounded.

This statement is ambiguous because it offers two possibilities: either the student or the bus had been grounded.

> I saw the student - in the bus that had been grounded.
> I saw the student in the bus - that had been grounded.

It is important for the purposes of the avoidance of ambiguity to show the noun which is doing the action; here it can be done by either introducing a word or two as in these;

> I saw the student in the bus who has been grounded
> (**who** links *I saw the student*, not to the bus, to the action).
> I saw the student in the bus which had been grounded
> (**which** links the bus, not the student to the action).

or the ambiguity can also be removed by changing the status of one of the nouns as in:

> I saw the students in the bus that were grounded
> (**were** links *I saw* to the action of the plural noun and not the singular)
> I saw the student in the bus that was grounded
> (**was** links *I saw* to the action of the singular noun and not the plural).

There are times though when the meaning of the individual words will be enough signal as to the actual meaning of the statement:

> I taught the student in the bus that was singing

In the above example there is no ambiguity because we normally think of people singing and not cars, although such a ridiculous alternative may tease the reader.

Ambiguity in Verb Clusters

Ambiguity can arise in verb clusters:

He protected the woman he loved with all his heart.

The questions that can arise out of this sentence are two. Did he protect the woman or love her with all his heart? Can you construct two sentences to show the two possible meanings that can be derived from the above sentence? Use the space below:

(a) ....

....

(b) ....

....

In the following pairs of sentences the first one is ambiguous while the second one is not. Can you explain why? Use the spaces provided after each pair:

The old fisherman mended the net at the beach.
The old fisherman mended the net while he was at the beach.

....

....

....

....

....

He polished the chair in the room in which she usually sat.
He polished the chair on the porch in which she usually sat.

....

....

....

....

....

....

Some Exercises on Ambiguities

Read the following sentences carefully; some of them are ambiguous while others are not. Mark the ambiguous ones A and the others U in the parenthesis provided after each sentence.

1. The faculty members we met now and then were very kind to us. ( )

2. The child hid the toy he found under his bed. ( )

3. The parents watched their children receive prizes proudly. ( )

4. I proudly watched my daughter perform a piano piece. ( )

5. The soldiers with the captives who were restless were ordered to behave themselves. ( )

6. Going towards the hall of residence the car hit the goat. ( )

7. The campus guards could not find the football equipment that had been stolen that morning. ( )

8. People who eat balanced diets seldom have health problems. ( )

9. She could not find the ladle to serve the punch which she had left on the dining table. ( )

10. Nobody tolerates people who whine all the time. ( )

11. Teenagers who stay out all night sometimes should be punished. ( )

12. Teenagers who stay out all night should seldom be punished. ( )

13. The head-porter has trouble with students who live in the hall all the time. ( )

14. The old lady spoke warmly to the naughty boy with a smile. ( )

15. The old lady spoke warmly to the naughty boy with the smile. ( )

16. With a smile on her face the old lady spoke warmly to the naughty boy. ( )

17. The old lady spoke to the naughty boy with the warm smile that she reserved for children. ( )

18. He spoke with the girl in the car that needed water. ( )

19. The men with the dogs that were barking were told to leave the queue. ( )

20. The men whose dogs were barking were told to leave the queue. ( )

More Exercises on Ambiguities

Each of the following sentences is ambiguous. In the spaces created below each sentence rewrite the sentence twice to show both meanings. You are at liberty to make the kinds of changes necessary to achieve clarity without drastically changing the meaning of the sentence. Write smooth, pleasing, grammatically correct sentences.

Example: A. I met a driver with a car that had no insurance.

Answers: I met a driver with a car which had no insurance.
I met a driver with a car who had no insurance.

Ambiguities and Dangling Modifiers 69

1. Tourists who visit the Slave Castles often break down and cry.

2. An advertising agent who had entered the conference hall briskly delivered a talk on lap-top computers.

3. The asafo company spotted the missing child with a basket of fruits that was going moldy.

4. The students were urged seriously to make the most of their University education.

5. We carefully washed the shells we had found in the sea.

   ....
   ....
   ....
   ....
   ....

6. At that party I spotted a guest with a smile that quickly captivated me.

   ....
   ....
   ....
   ....
   ....

7. They often went for a walk in the park that was their favorite site when the weather was good.

   ....
   ....
   ....
   ....
   ....

8. He sold the desk to the customer with carved legs and large drawers.

   ....
   ....
   ....
   ....
   ....

9. We were introduced to the manager with a lovely face that we found agreeable.

   ....

   ....

   ....

   ....

   ....

10. Lecturers of students who excel usually expect to be acknowledged.

    ....

    ....

    ....

    ....

    ....

Ambiguity in Pronouns

When the writer is not careful about the use of certain pronouns – especially the personal pronouns (he, she, it, they, etc.) and the demonstratives (this, that, these, those) – ambiguities can occur.

The personal and demonstrative pronouns function like nouns, except that these pronouns normally require antecedents. What this simply means is that a pronoun like **she** will not occur in writing unless a noun like **Adwoa** or **my daughter** or the **young woman** had previously occurred. Put another way, it will be confusing to hold a discussion in which the subject is only identified as **he**. There are times when the context will help to clarify the pronoun, as in a conversation when one speaker points to a man who just entered the room and remarks:

"He looks like our lecturer, doesn't he?"

And of course the conversation can go on indefinitely from this point without

.itifying the man who walked into the room. In the context of writing such an exception is not possible, and sooner than later the antecedent will have to be clarified. Remember that our concern lies with the academic essay and not with fiction were several rules can be broken and amended to suit the creative impulse.

The problem of ambiguity with the pronouns arises when a particular pronoun has more than one antecedent. Let us consider this statement:

> Mansa informed her sister that she would be late for the party.

In the larger context there will be no confusion because some statements would lead the reader to discover who is going to the party; but as it is, the statement is ambiguous because the personal pronoun **she** is preceded by two nouns, Mansa and her sister, either of whom might be the antecedent. There are a couple of ways in which the ambiguity may be eliminated:

> Mansa informed her sister that she (Mansa) would be late for the party.

This is perhaps the crudest way of solving the ambiguity. It is advisable at this stage in your academic progress to seek a more felicitous way of expressing yourself, as in:

> When the radio started the late night programme Mansa knew she would be late for the party.

> Mansa remarked that her sister would be late for the party

For the purposes of clarity it is advisable to start the construction with a noun so that the pronoun which follows may better be identified. In this respect, a sentence like:

> As I was patting the dog on the tail it hit me.

There is ambiguity because it is not clear whether the dog or the tail is doing the hitting. To avoid ambiguity we can construct the sentence this way:

> As I was patting the dog on its head it hit me with its paw.

The demonstrative pronouns *this, that,* etc., refer, quite properly, not to nouns but whole sentences or ideas expressed in verb clusters:

They have a very happy home life. That may account for the success in their careers.

As the sentences stand, it is perfectly clear that what may account for the success in their careers is their having a happy home life. You need to ensure that each time you use a demonstrative pronoun, the reference is clear.

Further Exercises on Ambiguities

Some of the following sentences contain examples of faulty references to pronouns while some do not. In the parenthesis provided at the end of each sentence indicate with the letter F the faulty ones and G the good ones.

1. He purchased a computer with software but it was not in a good condition. ( )

2. Her grandmother refused to pay her extra money though she was rich.
( )

3. Her grandmother refused to pay her extra money because she was rich. ( )

4. He called the man by his first name and handed him an envelope which was not surprising. ( )

5. He called me by my first name and handed me an envelope the contents of which did not surprise me. ( )

6. I was not surprised that he called me by my first name, neither did I find the contents of his letter surprising. ( )

7. Michael asked his brother if he had been invited to the party. ( )

8. Michael asked his brother if he wanted to go to the party. ( )

9. When the snake saw the cat it got frightened. ( )

10. He told the welfare officer that he did not know about the sanitary conditions in the hall of residence. ( )

11. She removed the diamond ring from the box and held it carefully to the light. ( )

12. Visitors are not expected to touch the animals at the zoo unless they are thoroughly examined. ( )

13. The doctor informed the technician that he had been fired from his job. ( )

14. The parents informed the teachers that they would have to show more responsibility. ( )

15. He spoke harshly to his father, but this could hardly have caused his heart attack. ( )

16. When her daughter was three years old, she decided to get married again. ( )

17. He showed me a picture of his family, but that was not what surprised me. ( )

18. Much as they are often caught up in immediate happenings, writers have constantly expressed in their works themes that are not confined to one place or time. ( )

19. The laboratory floor must be made suitable and under no condition must it become unsafe. ( )

20. In the University where I studied they were always encouraging students to excel. ( )

Each of the following sentences contains an ambiguity. On the lines provided re-write each sentence twice to remove the ambiguity and achieve clarity.

Example:
    A. He told his son that he was brilliant.
       He thought his son was brilliant.
       Kwadwo thought his son was brilliant and he told him so.

Ambiguities and Dangling Modifiers

1. The doctor told the patient that he looked good with gray hair.

2. The leaders informed the converts that they would have to fast for a week.

3. The tourist board decided to have the Slave Castle in the town painted because it was attracting many tourists.

4. The school prefect had to stay with the new student because she had been late.

5. The clown sang a song at the circus that amused the children very much.

6. When children are taken away from their day-care teachers they often look very happy.

7. The judge refused to give the armed robber a heavy sentence because he was such a nice man.

8. My father removed the pipe from its box and painted it carefully.

9. When Mr. Essuman caught his teenage boy smoking a cigarette, he tried to act naturally.

   ....

   ....

   ....

   ....

   ....

10. Kofi told Kwame that he would have to work very hard if he wanted to reach the top.

    ....

    ....

    ....

    ....

    ....

Dangling Modifiers

Dangling modifiers refer to the structural fault that can occur when the subject-predicate relationship is not clear; this absence of clarity is normally attributed to the misplacement of the sentence modifier. Let us consider this sentence:

> Moving towards the hall of residence, the goat hit the car.

The whole meaning of the verb cluster, **moving towards the hall of residence,** applies to the whole meaning of the sentence, pattern, **the goat hit the car,** hence the confusion. The connection between the verb cluster and the performer of the action is not clear because the subject-predicate relationship is lost. The sentence contains a dangling modifier – **moving towards the hall of residence** – because this verb cluster is not clearly attached to either of the nouns that come in close relation to it. Expressed in another way, our knowledge of normal English construction would lead us at first glance to take the goat as the performer of the action and thus have a meaning which sounds like: the goat was moving towards the hall of residence. Then knowing that the car rather than the goat is likely to move towards the hall of residence, the writer quickly corrects himself; what has happened here is that the writer has been momentarily led astray by a faulty construction. Here are some examples of dangling modifiers:

    Running into the room, her wedding date was announced.
Corrected: Running into the room, she announced her wedding date.

    Feeling feverish, a visit to the doctor seemed only logical.
Corrected: Feeling feverish, he thought he had better see a doctor.

    Visiting my landlord for the first time, his personality put me off.
Corrected: When I visited my landlord for the first time, his personality put me off.

How to Avoid Dangling Modifiers

Some modifiers dangle because of the wrong use of voice, as when the passive voice is used instead of the active construction in the sentence pattern.

Example: A result slip was seen **instead of** he saw a result slip.

 I am not suggesting that students should avoid using the passive construction altogether. The point I am trying to make is that they should be careful about its usage because it has the tendency to avoid identifying a clear subject for the action.
 Verb clusters in which the verb is a past participate also dangle sometimes:

    Quietly reading to himself, the squirrel quickly ran across his feet.

This sentence is written as if the cluster derived from the sentence, "The squirrel was quietly reading to himself". The sentence should read something like this: "The squirrel quickly ran across his feet as he was quietly reading to himself." Similarly, the following sentences contain dangling modifiers because the subjects, or the performers have not been clearly established in relation to the verb or the action:

    Having held discussions with my study-group on the topic, the exam was easy.

Corrected: I found the exam easy because I had held previous discussion on the topic with my study-group.

Publicly humiliated and voted out of office, his wife's heart was broken.
Corrected: Rejected by his family, he felt that life was not worth living.

The important point to note about correcting dangling modifiers is that it is not enough to have a subject or the performer of the action somewhere in the neighbourhood of the action; the subject must be clearly named as the one performing the action.

Verb cluster with "to" sometime dangle:

To understand slavery, the dominant ideology must be studied first.

It will be more grammatical to write:

To understand slavery, one must first study the dominant ideology.

Here the subject one has been introduced to clarify the subject of the action.

An adjective cluster may sometimes occur as a dangling modifier:

Furious at the delay, a riot nearly broke out.

As the sentence stands it appears as if the riot was furious, and since that is not the intended meaning one should write:

Furious at the delay, the spectators nearly started a riot.

Exercises on the Dangling Modifier

Some of the following sentences contain dangling modifiers, others do not. In the parenthesis provided after each sentence write D against the sentence with a dangling modifier and O against the sentence with no dangling modifier:

1. Angry at being snubbed by his subordinates again, a plan of revenge begun to grow in his mind. ( )

2. To become a first class business woman several tests must be passed. ( )

3. Not wishing to hurt her feelings he said he thought the dress was very nice. ( )

4. After leaving the hospital the student apparently wrote his impressions in a memo to the hospital board. ( )

5. Strolling down the beach from the western gate, Elmina Castle seemed very far away. ( )

6. Being irresponsible parents, nobody wanted to have anything to do with them. ( )

7. To understand how far we have come, we need to compare the state of the establishment to its previous one. ( )

8. The gate being locked, he shouted for the porter. ( )

9. Happy to have her with us again, Abena was given a hug by each one of us. ( )

10. Not having been detected early enough, Abena was given a hug by each one of us. ( )

11. Feeling hot and thirsty, the fresh coconut milk tasted very good indeed. ( )

12. By taking a nap before dinner, she was able to stay awake throughout the performance. ( )

13. Encouraged by the remarks of the critics, the young scholar decided to revise his paper for publication. ( )

14. When he finally summoned enough courage to visit Adehye Hall, his date was nowhere to be found.

15. Just to find a jug of water, she has to walk four miles everyday. ( )

16. Mindful of what had happened at the previous meeting, no invitation was sent to them. ( )

17. Cruising towards the driveway, that sports car was the most beautiful I had ever seen. ( )

    ....

    ....

    ....

18. To save a little more money, he walked to the lecture theaters each day. ( )

    ....

    ....

    ....

19. Already terrified by the thunder and the lightning, the appearance of the shadow set them screaming. ( )

    ....

    ....

    ....

20. Refused flatly by the porter, there was still a good chance of getting something out of the cleaner. ( )

    ....

    ....

    ....

More Exercises on the Dangling Modifier

Each of the following sentences contains a dangling modifier. In the spaces provided after each sentence revise each one in whatever way you consider best in order to remove the fault.

1. To appreciate the full significance of the project, some background information is necessary.

   ....
   ....
   ....

2. By working seriously for a semester, his grade point average improved considerably.

   ....
   ....
   ....

3. In setting the lyrics to music, a lot of changes have had to be made.

   ....
   ....
   ....

4. Unsure about the lady's reaction, he took a long time to propose marriage to her.

   ....
   ....
   ....

5. Happy about being called reliable, her readiness to co-operate was to be expected.

   ....
   ....
   ....

Ambiguities and Dangling Modifiers

6. Noticing that the child was coming to school without breakfast, the teacher sent for Araba's parents.

   ....
   ....
   ....

7. Not wishing to upset the young mother, the news about the death of her baby was at first withheld from her.

   ....
   ....
   ....

8. Suddenly realizing what they would be expected to do, it seemed best to withdraw their statement.

   ....
   ....
   ....

9. To create a cozy atmosphere for the hall dinner, candles were lit.

   ....
   ....
   ....

10. Having been punished twice by the discipline committee, a stiff sentence was to be expected.

    ....
    ....
    ....

Chapter 6

THE ACADEMIC ESSAY

Introduction

In this section we are going to discuss the components of the kind of essay you will be required to write at this stage in your academic career, Certainly this is not the first time you are going to write an essay; however, it is important to treat even the format of the essay with a little more seriousness than most students are inclined to do.

Usually the essay tests five main items:

(a) Your instructor is interested in how much information you have been able to assimilate in your course so far.

(b) Your control over the terminology used in your course will be evaluated in your essay.

(c) Another aim of the academic essay is to determine the student's understanding of and competence in manipulating the concepts and methodologies which have been introduced in the course.

(d) Your instructor will also show interest in your ability to demonstrate and apply research techniques (more on this in my next handbook).

(e) The use to which you put the information available is also going to be tested in your essay.

The Topic

Generally the topic for your essay would have been chosen for you by your instructor and the topic would usually accurately suggest the contents of the paper. However, before we discuss the details of the essay, we need to pay attention to the kinds of essay topics you are likely to deal with in the course of your undergraduate studies and sometimes beyond.

Sometimes the essay topic comes in the form of question as in the following example:

    i. How did the mountains and the sea affect the lives of the ancient Greeks?

ii. Can religion be defined?
iii. What is dispersal? How is it achieved in fruits?
iv. What is running?
v. Why do some commodities have higher price elasticity of demand than others?

Some essay topics would ask the students to provide a number of factors which would make a collective statement about the subject for discussion as in the following:

1. Outline the history of Christianity in Ghana from its inception to the end of the nineteenth century.

2. Outline the significance of the introduction of the alphabet for the development of literature.

3. Give a concise account of the importance of micro-organisms in agriculture.

4. As an executive, state and explain the steps you will take to ensure that your planning is effective.

5. Provide a brief description of the flight apparatus of Colombia sp.; and demonstrate how it differs from Struthio sp.

Other essay questions would demand of the student to study two items and highlight their similarities and differences as in:

1. Compare the principal beliefs and practices of Christianity with those of Islam

2. Compare and contrast the characters of Edna and Elsie in Chinua Achebe's *A Man of the People*.

3. What are the main differences and similarities between the CPP and UP in Ghana.

Most essay topics would ask the student to provide a discussion, as in:

1. Briefly discuss the adaptations shown by members of the order *Rodentia* (*Simplicidentata*) to their way of feeding.

2. Discuss the importance of upward communication in any organization.

3. "No one simple feature can be used to distinguish between a monocot and a dicot" Discuss.

4. Discuss the factors that affect resistance to diseases in man.

5. Discuss the nature and significance of planning in business administration.

Whatever form your topic takes, the essays you are going to write at this stage in your studies will require of you to provide an analysis even if the topic does not state specifically that you should analyse anything. An analysis asks for a critical look to be taken at the issues which you will raise in your paper. What this simply means is that your instructor is not going to be excited about a mere narration of events; rather, you should focus on evaluating the facts of your essay and on using these facts to make a statement about your topic if you are interested in getting a grade you will be proud to show in public.

Let us now consider other aspects of the procedure for writing the essay.

Before we do anything at all, we need to consider the topic we have to write on. This is an extremely important factor: that we read our topic and analyse it. Try to understand the topic by considering the kind of topic it is. Does the topic ask you to compare and contrast anything? If so, it means straight away that you will have to identify the two items involved in the discussion and take a close look at each item separately before you determine their similarities and differences. If you have a "discuss" question you should avoid a narration by all means; this point has been made already but it is important enough to warrant a repetition: such questions demand a critical evaluation of the details of the essay and an attempt to make a statement based on these facts.

After convincing yourself that you understand what is required of you, you may start to work on the essay. A word of caution! You do not start writing yet, although you might feel that you are ready to do so. As the "facts" keep coming to your mind do jot them down on a note pad because you need to arrange all these "facts" in a certain order; logic plays a very important role in essay writing. First you need to write an outline. An outline helps you to organize your thoughts and to establish an order in the way in which you arrange your thought. For the time being you can attempt an arrangement of your material into three broad areas to correspond to the following outline:

An Introduction
    (a) a definition of your terms or key words in the essay topic

(b) a thesis statement

(c) A methodology, or the items you intend to discuss and the desired order

A Body
       a detailed discussion of each of the items you listed under methodology

A Conclusion
    (a) a summary of the main ideas discussed in the work

    (b) a prediction or two, based on your findings.

The Introduction

The introduction works to demonstrate your understanding of the key words used in the essay topic, the purpose of the paper and the steps which you propose to apply in order to project your argument. From this definition it is clear that the introduction must consist of three parts which must be reflected in your outline.

    i. demonstrated understanding of the topic (definition of terms)
    ii. a thesis statement
    iii. methodology

How does one achieve this demand of the essay? Let us take each part and consider it for a while.

    A demonstrated understanding of the topic should be made evident in the first line or two of the essay. This section of the essay would be independent of the topic – in other words you are not required to copy out the topic in the first sentence of your essay; instead, you would use your own words to demonstrate your understanding of the topic. Try to avoid using the words in the topic, as much as possible. Of course you cannot avoid proper nouns but you can make evident by way of substitution, the use of synonyms and antonyms, your understanding of the terminology introduced in the course of your classes. This is a good time to consult your class notes and a good source book for your discipline, if you are writing outside examination conditions.

    Your thesis statement is important in imposing a controlling idea on the entire essay; it is that part of the essay which announces to your reader the essence of the essay. The thesis is the main idea around which all others should revolve and it is important to phrase it in the form of statement in order to distinguish the thesis from the topic. The thesis infers an argument, and it is important to grasp the persuasiveness inherent in the thesis concept. The statement will help you to clarify even to yourself what you intend to question, defend, prove or demonstrate in the paper.

Your methodology should tell your reader how you intend to proceed in your discussion; this part tells of the items you intend to deal with and in what order. The nature of your topic and the thesis you have in mind will shape the kind of method which your argument will follow.

The Outline for the Essay

We have paid attention to the introduction because it is important in helping you to arrive at a very good idea or what the topic demands of you. In this connection we are going to consider the outline which should further help you in organizing your ideas in a logical fashion. Having written your thesis statement, it is important to find the right way of supporting it, so as to achieve clarity. The outline allows you to have a view of the entire form of the paper even before you do actual "serious writing".

Some of you may never have worked with a written outline but have managed to pass your courses anyway, and as a result may feel that spending time writing an outline is a waste of time. I am not concerned in this manual with helping the student scrape through the course, but with passing well and with eliminating time wastage. If you insist, then I invite you to pass this test: How many combinations can you make of the following letters? In this test you must not use any writing or recording material; instead, you should recite your combinations, with no chances of repetition:

1. A and B? (You should have two combinations)

2. A, B, C ? (You should have six combinations)

3. A, B, C, D. ? (You should have twenty-four combinations)

Did you get stuck somewhere? Never mind, you are not alone; if you took this test with one hundred adults, you would have failed along with ninety-nine others!! The point which this "little" test makes is that even when we have in our heads all the ideas that we need to put in our essay, it is always a good idea to write them down, first in the order in which they come to our minds and then to attempt an arrangement of these ideas in a logical order, depending on the demands of our essay.

Supposing you have chosen a subject like student demonstrations to prove the thesis statement like this one:

> The purpose of this essay is to demonstrate that victory is not always worth the price it entails.

What are some of the ideas that will immediately come to mind to support it? You may need to identify some of the successes that students believe they chalk when they resort to demonstrations. The items in this section were collected from student responses when they were posed the problem. Four items will be sufficient for our purposes.

A. *Benefits*
    i.   – having a day of no lectures

    ii. – making their voices heard

    iii. – creating public awareness

    iv. – joining in the fun

These points will have to be arranged in an order which would either move from the least important to the most important or vice versa. Can you attempt that? I believe you can, so use the space below to arrange the points from what you believe to be the most important to the least important:

....

....

....

....

Now, let us turn to some of the sacrifices which the students feel they make when they embark on demonstration- eight items will do:

B. *Sacrifices*
    i.   – clashing with law-enforcement agents

    ii. – having rushed academic programmes

    iii. – spending unplanned holidays

iv. – risking government benefits

v. – annoying our parents

vi. – losing lives

vii. – disrupting academic calendars

viii. – weakening student solidarity

As with the successes, it is necessary to establish an order in this list in terms of importance or otherwise. You may try your hand by using the following spaces to rearrange the items here as you did with the benefits.

....
....
....
....
....
....
....
....

Here is what one student came up with for the first draft of an outline.

Thesis: The purpose of this paper is to prove that some of the time the benefits of student demonstrations are not worth the costs involved.

A. *Benefits*
   i. – joining in the fun

   ii. – having a day of no lectures

   iii. – creating public awareness

   iv. – making students' voices heard

B. *Costs*
   i.   – annoying our parents
   ii. – spending unplanned holidays
   iii. – weakening student solidarity
   iv. – disrupting the academic calendar
   v.   – risking government benefits
   vi. – having rushed academic programmes
   vii. – clashing with law enforcement agents
   viii.– losing lives

The twelve items will constitute twelve paragraphs. You will notice that we have used A and B to divide the entire essay into the two broad categories into which the discussion falls; that is, the successes and the sacrifices. Then we have used Roman numerals to identify the list of items we shall be dealing with. The next step is to try to find out the material we shall use to develop our paragraphs.

The outline is a guide; if in the course of searching for material to develop the paragraphs you find out that you are repeating yourself, then it means that you should merge some of the paragraphs which appear to be making very similar points. A good essay (written outside the examination room) has several crumbled sheets of writing and cancellations and rewriting and revision and editing behind it, so you do not need to despair, yet! But if you have a fair idea of what should go into the process as you are likely to do at the end of this handbook, then the process is much easier to handle. After you have completed such a step in an outline it is quite easy for you to see the direction in which you will cover. Can you think of the material you will need to develop these twelve items which will possibly cover twelve paragraphs? The partial sentences should act as guides for the heading by beginning with section A:

A. *Benefits*
   i.   – joining in the fun
   ii. – free bus rides into town
   iii. – singing and dancing
   iv. – carrying placards
   v.   – dressing very casually

Now, let us try to rearrange these points from the least important to the most important, bearing in mind our topic for the essay: *Victory is not always worth the price it entails.* You need to keep the item under Roman numeral 1. because that is going to act as the controlling or main idea of your thoughts in this paragraph. Remember that you are supposed to be working along with us in this exercise, so we expect you to have a note pad and a pen handy as you try your hands at paragraph composition. You are not likely to learn much if you do not make the effort. Do not presume that others arrived at these points listed against the lower case lettering without any effort – you obviously do not see it but you had better believe that we have spent a considerable amount of time on it, and so it is in perfect order if you find out that you are spending a lot of time trying to achieve similar results! After we had done the thinking and writing and rewriting and cancellations and crumbling or writing sheets, this is what we came up with:

A. *Benefits*
    i.   – joining in the fun
    ii. – dressing very casually
    iii. – free bus rides into town
    iv. – singing and dancing
    v. – carrying placards

These may be some of the ideas that may come to mind as one thinks of the topic for the first paragraph about having fun during student demonstrations. Can you think of others? Write yours in the order in which they occur to you as we have done with the four points above; then, try to rearrange them in order to achieve logic in the paragraph. You may start with the least important to the most important.

Keep what you have come up with on your note pad because it is as valid as ours. You will notice in the rearrangement that the material listed against lower case lettering a, b, c, d, has been indented from the upper case letter A. What this pattern means is that the further away the item is indented from the margin, the more subordinate role it plays in the paragraph. The further indented away from the margin an item is, the more subordinate role it plays in relation to the item that comes before it. In other words, '1. – joining in the fun' is the controlling or main idea of this paragraph, while items a, b, c, d, act as supports to the main idea. The supports play a subordinate role to the controlling idea.

Indeed, the ideas listed against the lower case letters can be further broken down to give an idea of what you intend to use to illustrate them, for example:

A. *Benefits*
   1. – joining in the fun
       a. – dressing very casually
           i. – shorts, hats, mismatch socks, masks

       b. – free bus rides into town
           i. – university buses, cars, trucks

       c. – singing and dancing
           i. – church songs with changed lyrics, profane songs

       d. – carrying placards
           i. – "If education is expensive, try ignorance"

An essential point about indention is that the further away the indention is made from the margin, the more subordinate role it plays in illustrating the controlling idea. In the above example, the item:

A. *Benefits*
1. – joining in the fun
    a. – dressing very casually
        i. – shorts, hats, mis-match socks, masks

will be used to throw light on the fact of dressing very casually which is an illustration of the idea of having fun, in itself a further illustration of the benefits which are derived when students embark on demonstrations. Therefore whereas joining in the fun' is the controlling idea of this paragraph, 'dressing very casually' acts as **major support** to the controlling, idea, with 'shorts, hats, mismatched socks, masks' performing the role of **minor support**.

At this point, we will leave you alone to develop the rest of this outline, by following the pattern we have provided, we believe you are ready to go on your own. The outline usually follows a pattern like this one:

A.
   1.
      a.
         i.
         ii.
      b.
         i.
         ii.

                B.
                    1.
                        a.
                            i.
                            ii.
                        b.
                            i.
                            ii.
                C.
                    1.
                        a.
                            i.
                            ii.
                        b.
                            i
                            ii.
                                            etc., etc.

In the next few pages we are going to show you the results of students who applied the outline to essay topics drawn from their own disciplines. None of the students had ever applied an outline to their work prior to the project; most had an idea about writing a plan, but it did not go beyond the broad demarcations of an introduction, a body and a conclusion. Certainly this is exactly where an outline begins, but we need something a little more elaborate than the following which a student wrote for an outline for a topic which demanded of him to discuss the characteristics of an ancient Greek religion:

Outline
Introduction: Why the Greek worshipped numerous gods.

Body: i.   The characteristics of the Greek gods.
      ii. Features of Greek religious practices.
      iii. Opposition to Greek traditional practices.

Conclusion: Adherents to polytheism and ascetimonotheism.

This student has some ideas of what an outline should look like, but this outline lacks detail and defeats its purpose of acting as a guide or a map to the entire essay. What do you think needs to be done here? Refer to the introduction to the outline at the beginning of this chapter and to the illustration with the topic about student demonstration in order to determine what you think can be done to remove the potential frustrations which are likely to arise if a student is stuck with such an outline. Here are a couple of examples by students who applied themselves diligently to the demands of the outline; we know you will fall into such a category as soon as you start and continue to make effort.

Topic
"A balanced sheet is a detailed statement of accounting equation". Explain.

Introduction
1. balance sheet = piece of information which shows the financial position of a firm
2. essay will discuss the importance of this balance sheet to the overall operations of a firm
3. paper will proceed by discussing two main areas of the balance sheet:
   (a) the assets
   (b) the liabilities.

Body
A. *Assets* – items of value owned by the firm

   1. properties of firm which have a longer period of life are known as fixed assets
      a. e.g. buildings, land, equipment and motor vehicles
   2. resources of the firm with a shorter period of life are called current assets
      a. e.g. stock, cash in hand, cash at bank, debtors.

B. *Liabilities* = debts that the business owes to its creditors
   1. Long term liabilities are debts that the business has to pay at a time which goes beyond the accounting year.
      a. long term loans

   2. current liabilities are debts to be met within the normal accounting period
      a. overdraft, accrued expenses and creditors

   3. capital is the amount provided by the owner of the firm
      a. seed money, shares

Conclusion
1. summary of assets and liabilities

2. implications of what the balance sheet does not reveal to the firm

Topic
Describe the factors which contribute to safety in the laboratory

Introduction
1. places equipped for experimental studies need protection

2. essay will point out some ways of preventing accidents at laboratories

3. some of the factors to be taken into consideration include atmospheric conditions, the provision of fire-fighting equipment, storage of chemcals, cleaning up of spillages, the provision of gas and water and the availability of a first aid box.

Body
1. atmospheric conditions
   a. it should be a uniform temperature
   b. it should be free from toxic gases, vapours and dust
   c. there should be an exhust system
   d. it should be cool, dry and moving
      i. extreme temperatures are dangerous to health and impair production

2. fire-fighting equipment and safety
   a. there should be fire extinguishers
   b. there should be a safe way of entering
      i. under normal circumstances
      ii. under emergency circumstances
   c. the doors should open outwards
   d. the corridors should be free from obstacles

3. storage of chemicals
   a. bench and side shelves should be provided
   b. inflammable solvents should be stored in fume hoods
   c. chemicals should be well labelled
   d. bottles should not be stored closely together
      i. some chemicals are easily oxidizable
      ii. other chemicals are highly oxidizing

4. spillages
    a. spill kits should be provided
        i. caustic spill kit
        ii. acid spill kit
        iii. spill control pillow
    b. floors should be free from spillages

5. gas and water supply
    a. there should be adequate and constant supply
    b. there should be no draw-off at any point

6. first aid box
    a. it should be within reach
    b. it should be fully equipped
    c. personnel should be trained

Conclusion
1. summary of factors that promote safety in laboratory
2. need to have government agencies constantly monitor laboratories

Topic
Give an account of the economic importance of plants

Introduction
1. flowering plants = plants which possess an enclosed seed
2. contribution of these plant to the economy
3. although they function as habitat for parasites, flowering plants are important for aesthetic purposes, provision of spices, industrial material, sources of medication, as cash-crop, and the provision of food and beverages.

Body
1. parasites
    a. grow and feed on other plants
        i. dodder and mistletoe
    b. habitat for pests
        i. worms and ants
    c. habitat for dead stems and leaves
        i. larvae and insects

2. aesthetics and shade

a. decoration
      i. roses and orchids
      ii. eucalyptus, flamboyant
3. spices
   a. flavouring of food
      i. cinnamon, cloves, garlic
   b. flavoring of medication
      i. mint
4. industrial material
   a. raw material
   b. cocoa – chocolate, soap, cream
   c. latex – rubber, plastic
   e. jute – jute bags
5. medication
   a. extracts from barks
      i. cinchona – quinine
   b. extracts from leaves
      i. penicillium notatum – penicillin
   c. opium – analgesic
6. cash crop
   a. timber, cocoa, pineapple
7. food and beverages
   a. primary producers
      i. grasses for domestic animals
      ii. plankton for fishes
   b. food as sources of energy
      i. carbohydrates – cereal, sugarcane, millet
   c. sources of protein
      i. beans
   d. sources of vitamins and oils
      i. spinach, groundnut
   e. sources of fruit
      i. mangoes, oranges
   f. sources of beverages
      i. cocoa, tea, coffee

Conclusion
1. benefits far outweigh cost of flowering plants
2. to encourage people to grow more flowering plants around buildings

Topic
What factors promoted Pan-Hellenism in ancient Greece?

Introduction
1. The nationalistic feeling of belonging together among the ancient Greeks = pan Hellenism
2. essay to take a critical look at the factors which helped to foster this feeling of oneness
3. the five main factors to be discussed are their common descent, language, religion, their athletics festivals and their respect for human dignity.

Body
1. common ancestry
   a. Hellens
      i. Hellen's three sons - Aeolus, Dorus, Ion
      ii. descendants called Aeolic, Dorians and Ionians

2. common language
   i. dialects were Aeolian, Dorian and Ionian

3. religion as a binding force
   a. common belief in principal gods and goddesses
      i. Apollo, Athena, Artemis

4. love for athletics festivals
   a. most important of festivals were Olympian games for Zeus
      i. most esteemed of all games

5. respect for human dignity
   a. promotion of intellectual growth
      i. group of philosophers in Greece
   b. high quality of human relations

Conclusion
1. summary of five contributing factors
2. implications of example of Greece to new democracies

Topic
Discuss the physiological importance and uses of water in plants.

Introduction
1. water as a universal solvent
2. paper to discuss water as a medium for life
3. essay will proceed by discussing the property of water as a good solvent and its effect on cell growth.

Body
A. a universal solvent
    1. physiological importance of water
        a. promotes cell growth
        b. promotes photosynthesis

    2. uses of water
        a. activates enzymes
        b. regulates temperature
        c. assists in fertilization
        d. provides supports

B. cell growth
    1. in plants and animals
        a. cell division
        b. cell enlargement
        c. cell elongation

    2. prevention of desiccation
        a. root permeability
        b. salt accumulation

    3. provision of support
        a. turgidity in herbaceous plants

Conclusion
1. influence of water as a solvent and on cell growth

2. implications of water deficit to crop production in some ecological zones.

    You are advised to get into the habit of writing an outline before you start writing your essays because an outline helps you to have a good opportunity to put your thoughts on paper and do all the canceling and adjustment necessary before you proceed. It is quite normal to wonder how all of this is going to work under the usual tense conditions unleashed by the examinations climate. But that is precisely the point! You need to get your thoughts so organized as to eliminate that tension; preparing adequately for an examination implies being in control of the situation and getting your facts well organized.

Certainly, there is no rule about the number of paragraphs you should have in an essay or the number of items you should employ to support your paragraphs; it all depends on the length of the essay and how much you have to say about that one idea which the paragraph is supposed to carry. However, it is useful to be as precise as you can manage it. In the next chapter we shall deal with the paragraph in some detail.

Chapter 7

PARAGRAPHING

In this section we are going to discuss some of the demands of paragraph writing. Much as we are aware that you have always been writing paragraphs, it pays to pay attention to paragraphs in this handbook because paragraphs are what we write most often; after all, the essay is a string of paragraphs. At this point we invite you to revise the first chapter to this handbook where we discussed the characteristics of a paragraph. In the chapter our main concern was to guide your reading of the paragraphs; here we are going to attempt to write paragraphs.

What the paragraph in your essay is supposed to do is to take up the ideas which you have listed at the end of your introduction and which you have fleshed out in your outline and develop them to support the main thesis statement for the entire essay. As you can already see, composing the paragraph requires more than simply indenting the next line. It is helpful to consider the paragraph a miniature composition with the following attributes:

1. presentation of one main idea
2. thoughts conveyed must have connection to the main idea of essay
3. continues to reveal main idea by lending support and illustration
4. may raise some limitations of that idea

Let us try and compose a paragraph from one of the ideas we came up with as we drew up an outline for the paper on student demonstrations. Let us choose the one about dressing very casually:

1. Some of the students who decided to go out and demonstrate against a decrease in student loans did so because they were bored by the routine of university life.

2. Their desire to have fun was so great that it showed even in the way they dressed for the occasion.

3. While a lot of the students came out in shorts of all standing – rather unusual despite the weather – others wore various headbands, hats with or without feathers, and I actually saw some of the male students in women's head scarves (talk about equality !)

4. The determination to draw attention to themselves and provoke humour

could also be seen in the deliberate effort to wear socks which did not match and to cover their faces with grotesque masks.

You can see that the main idea in this paragraph has been to underscore the idea of having fun during student demonstration by focusing on the use of attire. The sentences have been so composed as to carry that main idea. If you read this paragraph very carefully you will realize that the first sentence has set the tone for the rest of the paragraph by highlighting the idea of having fun. This sentence carries the main idea or theme for the paragraph, and it is known as the theme sentence for the paragraph; every well-written paragraph must have a theme sentence. Can you attempt a sentence analysis of this paragraph? If you are not very sure of what is required of you, please revise chapter one of this handbook for directions.

The functions of paragraphs are diverse; however, the following are some of the roles a paragraph can play in an essay:

> announce an introduction
> as in:

Plant without leaves, flowers or green colouring matter, and which grow on other plants or decaying matter are called fungi. The cells of fungi are very small and possess discrete membrane-bounded nuclei. Even though there are unicellular forms, most of these cells are filamous. A concern of this paper is to discuss the advantages and disadvantages of fungi to living organisms. Fungi are disadvantageous to man because they destroy food, cause foot-rot, produce ringworm, destroy industrial equipment and pollute water. However, fungi are useful in fertilizing the soil and serving as sources of food. The advantages of fungi include their industrial use for baking and brewing medicine and for the manufacture of organic substances.

Can you identify the parts of this introduction? Please do so because you are about to compose one for yourself and you need to refresh your mind about what an introduction to an academic essay should look like.

Write an introduction in the spaces provided about your hall of residence:

....

....

....

....
....
....
....
....
....

      identify a problem
      as in:

    Some flowering plants produce substances which are dangerous to man and his environment. The marijuana plant produces an alkaloid known as canibito. The canibito induces a neurotic effect on the user and it oftentimes leads to mental disorders. Another plant called allelopathy secretes alkaloids which prevent other plants from growing in its vicinity. The interference of man's thinking faculty by marijuana and the inability of other plants growing near to a specific flowering plant show some of the detrimental effects of flowering plants to man and his environment.

Write a paragraph which identifies the problem of drug abuse in the spaces provided below:

....
....
....
....
....
....
....
....

compare and contract
as in:

Psychology is very close in its endeavours to the natural sciences in the sense that both disciplines are based on empirical findings as opposed to opinions or beliefs. Other attributes of psychology like repeatability, predictability and inference indicate that psychology, like science, is based on a systematized knowledge acquired through careful observation. However, there is a marked difference between the two disciplines in the area of measurement. The things that psychology tends to measure – human behaviour, prestige, self-esteem, intelligence and the subconscious – do not lend themselves for measurement as easily as finding the weight of a specimen or the dimensions of a table as it exists in the other sciences. As a result, whereas measurement in the natural sciences is absolute, psychological measurements are always relative.

Write a paragraph which compares life in the dormitory of a secondary school to life in a hall of residence:

....

....

....

....

....

....

....

....

tell a story
as in:

Before the birth of my first child my wife insisted that the baby should be properly outdoored and according to her she would invite all our friends and relatives to come and celebrate the birth of the

child. I, however, told her that I was not going to perform any such ceremony because I was heavily in debt. This resulted in a heated argument with my wife calling me a miser and accusing me of reducing her to a laughing stock. When I was summoned before my in-laws I knew I was in for trouble.

Write a paragraph which tells of the most embarrassing moment of your life:

....

....

....

....

....

....

....

....

draw a conclusion
as in:

Therefore rodents, like other herbivores, can eat any type of herbivorous diet be it solid or liquid, because of their modified features and dentition. Besides, the modified features which enable them to dig, climb and jump are not only used in search of food in the soil or up the tree, but also, they serve as protective adaptations. In this vein, the rat digs numerous long holes in the soil to serve as a home while the squirrel lives on trees for most of its life. The natural endowments of animals should always be taken into consideration when making plans which centre around them.

Write a conclusion to a debate which took place in the hall about the use to which SRC dues should be put:

....

....

....
....
....
....
....
....

A paragraph may be composed to do more things than we have tried to do together; for example, a paragraph can make a proposition, draw an analogy, show causes and effects, define a problem, call for action, solve a problem, etc. etc. etc. But whatever specific role a paragraph plays, it always develops an idea. What this means is that the paragraph moves in a certain direction as it carries its message in its sentences.

Patterns of Development

There are various ways in which a paragraph can be developed. These include the direct, the pivoting and the suspended methods of pattern development. In this hand/workbook we are going to concentrate on the first method of paragraph development which is the direct pattern. We have specifically chosen this method because it is the method which is most often used in academic writing and, perhaps more than the others, it lends itself more easily to clarity.

The Direct Pattern

In the first chapter of this book where we discussed the art of reading we paid a lot of attention to the first sentence and concluded that it usually holds the key to the rest of the paragraph. When the theme sentence or topic sentence is located at the beginning of the paragraph we say that, that paragraph has followed the *direct pattern*. In developing your paragraphs for your essays you only need to go to the outline for the essay and pick out those items which you propose to discuss and construct your sentences around those ideas.

Let us consider this paragraph together:

Consequently, the methods employed in teaching a subject and

its evaluation depend both on the nature of the subject itself and the teacher. The teacher can teach by lecturing. With this method the students become the recipients of knowledge and have very little chance of contributing to the exercise. When the teacher decides to adopt a method based on discussion, he can pose a problem, sit back and allow the students to express their views on the problem. The review method usually deals with going over a lesson which has already been taught by bringing to light the most important aspects of that lesson.

Read the first sentence again and try to find out that one idea which the paragraph proposes to talk about. What is the idea here? Underline it, and then underline subsequent references to it in the following sentences. You must have remembered how we went about learning how to extract the meaning out of a written paragraph. The process is the same with the composition, and this time you want to make sure that your reader understands you clearly.

Sometimes a paragraph is so long that the theme sentence comes in the second sentence as opposed to the first. We recommend strongly that you place your theme sentences at the beginning of your paragraphs in order to have a direct hold on your ideas.

Read the following paragraphs and after identifying the topic noun find out the roles the rest of the sentences are playing in the rest of the paragraph:

The first stage in the production process, stage 1, is defined to cover the phase of production when the average product is rising for every increase in the variable input. It covers the level of production up to the point at which the average product reaches its maximum.

Furthermore, the cost of acquiring a fixed asset must be considered when assessing and allocating depreciation. The total cost of a fixed asset will include the invoice price of the asset. After the acquisition of an asset, for instance, plant and machinery, there is the need to transport it to its required location. The cost incurred in bringing the asset to its required location must be regarded as an integral part of the total cost of the asset. Similarly, costs of installing the asset and setting it up for use can also be properly included as part of the total cost of the asset. Thus, if the invoice price of the plant and machinery is 5000 cedis, the cost of transporting it to the factory is 1000 cedis and the cost of installation and setting up for use is 1200 cedis, the total cost of the plant and machinery will be 7200 cedis.

The third factor which led to the deposition of Iyasu was his support of

Germany and Turkey during the first world war. Germany and Turkey were enemies of Ethiopia, and these two countries were on the same side of the war. On the other side of the war were Britain and France. As a result of this arrangement the Ethiopian nobility expected Iyasu to support Britain and France in this war. However, Iyasu supported the other side because of his affairs with Turkish and German women. This position was seen by the nobility as a betrayal of loyalty and in 1916, Iyasu was deposed and excommunicated.

Exercise on the Paragraph

Using the following theme sentences, write paragraphs of four sentences in the spaces provided below:

The problem facing the undergraduate student in this country are solvable.

....
....
....
....
....
....

One disturbing factor about this hall of residence is the high noise level.

....
....
....
....
....
....

Perhaps we should start by talking about improving our sanitary conditions.

....

....

....

....

....

....

One wonders if the authorities really understand the importance of having a functional library in the hall ....

....

....

....

....

....

It will surprise you to know that some students have no idea about the festivals in their villages ....

....

....

....

....

....

In order to find out if your paragraph has unity it must be consistent in its handling of the one idea which paragraph is supposed to concern itself with, it must avoid digression and make sure that all the sentences are saying something about the topic noun.

Paragraphs may be described as a string of beads, each connected to the other. You may read the paragraphs which we used to illustrate the direct method, and you will notice that although each has its own coherence the theme sentences read as if they have other ideas in mind, because the first few words refer to an earlier point or have hints of what points may precede the ones being discussed. These indications speak to the relationship which exists between the paragraphs. Some connecting words are important in showing the transition which occurs between paragraphs. Before we use those connecting words we should always pause and find out the relationship which exists between the two paragraphs which are being connected. This is important in avoiding using the same word to begin each paragraph. Imagine what an essay would read like if every paragraph began with "furthermore"!!

Some of these transitional words may occur under more than one heading because it can function in more than one way.

Time or Place
until now,
at the same time,
subsequently,
above,
below,
later, etc

Restatement
in other words,
to restate,
in simpler terms,
to express it differently, etc.

Sequence
in the first place,
secondly,
finally, etc.

Insistence
indeed, yes,
in fact, etc.

Amplification
furthermore,
also,
in addition,
again,
further, etc.

Consequence
accordingly,
therefore,
hence,
as a result,
then, etc.

Likeness
similarly,
likewise, etc.

Contrast
on the contrary,
on the other hand,
but,
however, etc.

Chapter 8

COMPOSING THE INTRODUCTION AND THE CONCLUSION

The Introduction

Let us, together, try and compose a couple of introductions. These exercises will be based on topics drawn from various subject areas. Suppose you had a topic like this one from the natural sciences:

> With relevant examples discuss the view that nomenclature is important to man

The topic has at least one word, "nomenclature" which ought to be defined right at the beginning. Having looked up this key word preferably by reading over your notes and by consulting a dictionary of botany, you may proceed to rewrite this topic in your own words. What we will be providing are only examples; they are not model answers upon which the student is expected to improve. Rather, the challenge is for the reader to follow the directives and attempt a definition of his or her own. Having gone through the process as outlined above you may end up with a statement like this:

> The application of correct names to individuals, plants or organisms is of significance to the student of Botany. The method by which names are assigned is determined by the international code of botanical nomenclature.

These sentences show the reader the student's understanding of the key word in the topic, nomenclature. It also shows that the writer has not just blindly copied the definition from a secondary source but that he has linked the definition to other parts of the essay topic about the importance of nomenclature to man. The sentences in capital letters show us that the writer has also tried quite hard to avoid repeating the words in the topic. Should the writer now use the word" nomenclature" in the course of the essay the instructor would have a clear idea of the student's understanding of the terminology employed in the course.

The second part of the introduction, as we have already stated, should tell us what you intend to achieve in the paper. The thesis statement answers the questions: why am I writing this paper? What I am I trying to prove? Using the same topic about the importance of nomenclature to man, we may end up with a thesis statement which reads like the following:

> The purpose of this paper is to discuss the role which nomenclature plays in the study of plant taxonomy.

You will notice that this writer has indicated the limitations of his or her scope of enquiry to plant taxonomy.

The methodology should provide a list of items you intend to discuss in your paper and in what order. Working on the same paper the methodology might appear like this:

> The discussion will proceed by considering the importance of nomenclature in establishing uniformity, in serving as a reliable system of naming plants, in giving precise names to plants and, finally, in avoiding ambiguity in the naming of plants.

The introduction to the topic, *With Relevant Examples Discuss the View that Nomenclature is Important to Man,* may appear in the following form:

> The application of correct names to individuals, plants or organisms is of significance to the student of Botany. The method by which names are assigned is determined by the international code of botanical nomenclature. The purpose of this paper is to discuss the role which nomenclature plays in the study of plant taxonomy. The discussion will proceed by considering the importance of nomenclature in establishing uniformity in naming plants, in serving as a reliable system of naming plants, in giving precise names to plants and finally in avoiding ambiguity in the naming of plant.

Can you identify the three parts of the introduction in the above paragraph? I believe you can do it. Just give yourself a chance.

Let us consider another example together:

EXPLAIN THE RELEVANCE OF HOME ECONOMICS TO A COLLEAGUE IN ANOTHER DEPARTMENT

Can you identify the key words in this topic? The key words are those words from which the entire topic appears to derive special importance. In this topic the key words are obviously "home economics". Having identified the key words the next step is to try to write down your own understanding of the words. As in the previous example the student who is interested in making a good grade will read over his lecture notes in order to find out how the words have been defined in class. Apart from this source you also need to consult a good source book on Home Economics which would provide perhaps a more detailed definition of the subject than your instructor would have had time to provide in class. Do bear in mind that your lecture hours are usually inadequate to provide all the information you require and with reason: you are expected to make friends with the library. After the reading and cross-checking from other sources have been done you may end up with a sentence like the following:

> Contrary to popular misconceptions that it is a subject which deals only with cooking and sewing, home economics is a field of study that draws its knowledge from its own research as well as from other disciplines, especially the natural and social sciences. Home economics has the broad aim of improving the quality of family life in particular and human life in general.

Do you remember what comes after the definition of terms in the introduction? Certainly! This is the time we announce the purpose of the essay by declaring a thesis statement which, for a topic such as the one we are dealing with, may sound like this:

> The aim of this essay is to discuss the relevance of home economics to family life and relationships.

After the thesis statement you will have to indicate the areas with which you plan to concern yourself in your discussion, and the order in which these areas will appear in the body of the essay. A sentence such as this one will be adequate:

> The relevance of home economics may be seen in its definitions, assumptions, aims and objectives and, finally, in its concerns.

The introduction to the topic, EXPLAIN THE RELEVANCE OF HOME ECONOMICS TO A COLLEAGUE IN ANOTHER DEPARTMENT, may read like this paragraph:

> Contrary to the popular misconception that it is a subject which deals with cooking and sewing, home economics is a field of study that draws its knowledge from its own research, as well as from other disciplines, especially the natural and social sciences. Home econo-

mics has the aim of improving the quality of family life in particular and human life in general. The aim of this essay is to discuss the relevance of home economics. We shall pay attention to its definitions, assumptions, aims and objectives and, finally, its concerns.

Illustrations of the Introduction

A group of students drawn from varied disciplines were invited to take part in a project which promised to make them more sensitive to the demands of the essay. In the rest of this section we are going to show you four examples of the effort of these students who applied the techniques of writing the introduction to their own writing. You will notice that there are two versions of each introduction. The "first version" refers to the introduction the student wrote at the beginning of the project, before being introduced to the content of the exercise. The "revised version" refers to the end product of the effort to write introductions by applying such techniques like the definition of the terms, the thesis statement and the methodology. We have avoided making major editorial changes, in order to preserve the form and content of the students' actual efforts. Please read these versions very carefully, and try to identify the three main parts of the introduction in the revised version; the whole point is to show you that when the technique is applied some remarkable results are achieved.

Topic
Discuss how Religion helps humans to adjust to the stressful reality of death.

First Version
There are many ways in which humans can use their religion to overcome the sorrows, suffering and frustration imposed by the loss of other human beings they love so much. The aim of this essay is to discuss how man's religion can be of help when one becomes terribly disturbed and confused as a result of human loss. In such situations the individual requires explanation for his conditions. These explanations can be found in the unpredictability and uncontrollability of death by man, one's religious beliefs about death, the question of life after death, the concept of reincarnation, some religious customs and rites for the dead.

Revised Version
There are many ways in which humans can employ their belief in the supernatural to overcome the sorrow, suffering and frustration imposed by the loss of a loved one. The concern of this essay is to discuss how religion can be of help when one becomes terribly disturbed as a result of this loss. Some of

these sources of help can come in the form beliefs about death, the question of life after death, religious rites for the dead and as well, the unpredictability and uncontrollability of death.

Topic
Explain why mathematics has several definitions. Illustrate your answer with specific examples.

First Version
Mathematics, as a discipline, is as old as man. Many philosophers who were concerned with the study of mathematics concluded that mathematics is a discipline which penetrates all other domains of human study and serves as a model of all intellectual enterprises – economics, social sciences and very largely the natural sciences. It has therefore been variously described as "the queen of all subjects" "the language of science" and "the mirror of civilization" by which man creates and discovers theories to solve present and future problems. Thus it has no unique definition.

Revised Version
Mathematics refers to that discipline which penetrates all other domains of human study and which serves as a model for all intellectual enterprises. Perhaps the various known descriptions of mathematics and the multiplicity of its function make it rather difficult to come up with one definition which will be acceptable to everyone. The purpose of this essay is to discuss three main reasons why mathematics has varying definitions: first we shall discuss its long history, then we shall consider its relation to other fields of human study and, finally, we shall discuss its abstract nature.

Topic
"Provision for the depreciation of fixed assets having a finite useful life should be made by allocating the depreciable cost of the assets as fairly as possible to the periods expected to benefit from their use". Briefly explain the factors to be taken into consideration in relation to the above statement.

First Version
Depreciation may be defined as the permanent and continuing diminution in the quality, quantity of value of an asset. In the statement of *Standard Accounting Practice 12 (SSAP), Accounting for Depreciation,* depreciation is defined as "the measure of the wearing out, consumption or other loss of value of a fixed asset whether arising from use, effluxion of time, obsolescence, through technology and market changes."

Revised Version
Fixed assets reduce in quality, quantity or value through use or the passage of time. The duration of the useful life of fixed assets is limited. When that asset is finally put out of use, that part of the cost that is not recovered on disposal is called depreciation. Depreciation therefore is that part of the cost of the fixed asset which is consumed during its period of use by the firm. Causes of depreciation are physical deterioration, economic factors, time factors, and depletion. These causes will be analyzed in the light of acquisition costs, the estimated useful life and the estimated residual value.

Topic
Give an account of the political structure of Sparta and describe the nature of its government.

First Version
Sparta was one of the city-states in Greece. Her citizens settled in the valley of Laconia along the River Eurotas. The constitution of her political set-up was supposed to have been created by a law-giver called Lycurgus. Her political structure was divided into four parts, namely, the Diarchy, the Gerousia, the Apella and the Ephorate.

Revised Version
The different components of a ruling system in a country form what is known as her political structure, while the body in charge of running its administration is called the government. The purpose of this study is to identify and examine the main parts of Sparta's political structure, and its functions in an effort to describe the type of government it had. We propose to proceed by looking at the four major parts of this structure, mainly the Diarchy, the Gerousia, the Apella and the Ephorate.

The best way in which you will progress in this segment of your essay is to practice constantly. Find out from the department and the library past questions in your areas of study and try to compose introductions for them. After the introduction try to compose an outline for that topic.

The Conclusion

The conclusion to the essay is made up of two parts: the first deals with a *summary* of the ideas discussed in the essay, while the second makes a statement out of your findings in such a way as to *suggest* other *ways* of tackling the problem discussed in the essay. The second part of the conclusion need not be as long as the summary. Indeed a sentence or two will suffice.

If we were to write on the essay topic in chapter six – do you remember the one about the price of victory which we used to demonstrate an outline? – we might have a conclusion like this one:

> This essay has demonstrated that when students embark on demonstrations the sacrifices they make far outweigh the benefits. For example, whereas the students have a sense of achievement which ranges from having a little fun, creating a holiday for themselves, getting public attention through to educating the public on some vital issues, some very important sacrifices are made in this endeavour. Some of the sacrifices include harsh criticism from some parents, wasting a lot of time at home, weakening student solidarity and causing the planned academic year to undergo unwanted changes. The more serious sacrifices are that when students go on demonstrations they risk losing indispensable government support for education, and even when this does not happen the academic year is usually completed under pressure. Perhaps clashing with law enforcement agents and sometimes losing the lives of students and members of the public make one wonder about the effectiveness of student demonstration as a method of seeking redress. In order to avoid such resort to unconventional ways of making its point the student body should be sensitized to the nation's priorities and be actively encouraged to see itself as an ally, not an enemy of government.

The first part of this conclusion has summarized the points in the outline, while the last sentence which goes beyond the summary has made a suggestion about the possibility of preventing the occurrence of student demonstrations. Such a suggestion could form the basis of another paper.

The following examples of conclusions were drawn from the attempts made by students who participated in the project. As in those used to illustrate the introductions, the first version refers to the student's own effort without the format for writing the conclusion while the revised version is the end product of the application of the two parts of a conclusion to their writing. Please read the two versions of each topic carefully, and try to determine where the summary ends and where the prediction begins.

Topic
Give an account of the political structure of Sparta and describe the nature of its government.

First Version
From the above discussion, it can be said that each part of the Spartan political

structure had a distinct role to play. Therefore, given the different parts that constituted this structure, one can conclude that the Spartan government was a mixed one.

Revised Version
The four distinct parts of the Spartan political structure played diverse but important roles in the formation of her government. Given the different components of this structure, it can be deduced that the system was a mixed one. However, the kind of system established by Sparta did not make room for the active participation of every adult citizen in the running of the city-state. It was a government that favoured the rich and the nobility class which was at the helm of affairs. In view of all these facts one wonders whether any of the Greek city-states like Athens could also have adopted this kind of system. Looking at the political trends of the contemporary world it is doubtful if any country would embrace such a system.

Topic
Summarize the major experiments that led to the discovery of the subatomic particles.

First Version
The subatomic particles, protons, electrons and neutrons were discovered through experiments carried out by William Crooke, J. J. Thompson and Chadwick respectively.

Revised Version
The key investigations that led to the awareness, for the first time, of the constituents of the smallest particle of an element were carried out by William Crooke, J.J. Thompson and Chadwick. Their analysis established that an atom consists of three basic components, namely, the electron, the proton and neutron. The particles were discovered in three different experiments which are the cathode ray tube experiment and the nuclear reaction experiment. In an atom the protons and neutrons occupy the nucleus with the electrons surrounding the nucleus.

Topic
Summarize the major experiments that led to the discovery of the subatomic particles.

First Version
This paper has taken a critical look at the key investigations that led to the discovery of the subatomic particles carried out by William Crooke, J. J. Thompson and Chadwick. Their analysis established that an atom consists of

three basic components, namely, the electron, the proton and the neutron.

Revised Version
Therefore, whether in the gaseous, liquid or solid state, matter contains three basic subatomic orbitals namely proton, electron and neutron, as the experiments discussed in this paper have shown. The properties of these particles contribute to the electrical neutrality of matter as a whole. But in all these experiments the only state which was considered was the gaseous state; as a result, it is possible to make some modifications in the experimental set-up to enable further studies to be conducted into the properties of the subatomic particles in the liquid and solid states. Such an effort could lead scientists to discover whether the characteristics of protons, electrons and neutrons contribute to the various states of matter, apart from the intermolecular forces with the various states.

Having seen for yourself the result which can be achieved when you make the effort, we strongly urge you to emulate these examples and get better grades than you have been getting. Remember that things can always get better.

Chapter 9

PUNCTUATION

If we listen very carefully when others speak, we will notice that they sometimes pause or change their tone. If such speeches were rendered in writing, the pauses and changes in tone would indicate various forms of punctuation. Certainly we cannot rely completely on our senses to discover the times we need to employ our punctuations; for example, no amount of good listening skills will allow any of us to determine when an apostrophe or a quotation mark is supposed to occur. The kind of punctuation used in a sentence is largely determined by the structure of that sentence. Some of the most common forms of punctuation in writing are the following:

    comma (,)
    semi-colon (;)
    colon (:)
    quotation marks (" " or ' ')
    apostrophe (')
    parenthesis (( ) or [ ])
    question mark (?)
    full stop or period (.)

Comma (,)

Perhaps the comma is the most frequent mark of punctuation used within the sentence, and at the same time it is the most frequently misused. The comma is usually used to separate items in the sentence from each other; these items may be words, phrases or clauses; in this respect the comma plays a role similar to that of the dash, the parenthesis, the colon and semi-colon. Here are a few guidelines on the use of the comma:

> A comma or a semi-colon may be used to separate independent clauses joined by **and, or, but, for** and similar coordinating conjunctions.

The sentence, "You will have to pay the fine, and then we'll think of what to do next" is called a compound sentence because the two clauses joined by the coordinating conjunction are independent. What this means is that the group of words on either side of "and" can stand on their own as complete sentences, as in:

> You will have to pay the fine. Then we'll think of what to do next.

The independent clauses are separated by a comma because they are joined by a coordinating conjunction. The semi-colon may be used when **and** is omitted:

> You will have to pay the fine; then we'll think of what to do next.

Use commas to set off names and similar words in direct address. Let us consider these two sentences:

> I am calling, Mummy, to say that I will be home this weekend.
> I am calling Mummy to say that I will be home this weekend.

The difference in the sentence is marked by the use of commas in the first and their absence in the second. The first sentence, punctuated by the commas, sets off the word **mummy** as the person to whom the speaker is addressing the information, while the second makes mummy the indirect object of the verb **calling,** and as such the information is directed at someone else.

Use commas to separate elements in a series.

> In that tro-tro bus were people, luggage, goats, fresh fish, and firewood.

> On my son's desk you are likely to find books, pencils, crayons, erasers, pieces of paper, and toys.

Use a comma before and after direct quotations and to set off **he said** and similar attributions.

> "We are indeed lucky to have such a team leader," remarked Kwabena.

> Kwabena remarked, "We are indeed lucky to have such a team leader."

When the attribute precedes the quotation, as in the second sentence, the colon may be used:

> Kwabena remarked: "We are indeed lucky to have such a team leader."

Use a comma to separate items which suggest a contrast or a choice.

> I am drowning, not waving.
>
> She drinks wine, not beer.
>
> My husband would rather fly, not travel by boat.

Use a comma to separate names of places, addresses and items in dates.

> The Slave Castle at Elmina, Ghana, bears testimony to a terrible fact.
>
> Mount Saint Helen exploded in The State of Washington, United States of America.
>
> I live at 45 Kakum Close, University of Cape Coast.
>
> My son was born on October, 1, 1980.

Use the comma to separate an introductory phrase or adverbial clause from the main clause.

> Armed with the facts about his good performance at the University, I attended the meeting of the awards committee.
>
> Impressed by her thorough analysis of the problem, her supervisor awarded an A grade for the paper.
>
> When he comes, tell him I had to leave immediately.

Use commas to set off forms of the appositive.

> My children have an appointment with Dr. Lee, the dentist.
>
> Please give the result slip to Kay, the administrative secretary.

Use commas to set off non-restrictive modifiers.

> The nun, who takes care of abandoned babies, has been transferred to another region.
>
> University faculty members, who represent a group of intellectuals anywhere, must assist their governments.

Exercises on the Comma

Instructions: insert commas at the appropriate places in the following sentences:

1. I complained to my counsellor about the behaviour of my roommate and he advised that I talk directly to him about how I feel.

2. The hawker would have liked to sell her wares inside the hall but the porter told her she could not.

3. Walking through the park I heard some people practising how to speak in tongues while others were singing praying or listening.

4. Due to the massive turn-out of spectators the football match between Casely-Hayford Hall and Commonwealth Hall was very exciting.

5. Next Friday evening new members of the Students' Representative Council will be sworn in.

6. When you are in secondary school the idea of a university can sound intimidating.

7. The Vice Chancellor of a university must be given the right to appoint his deans who must have the appropriate academic and administrative qualifications and experience to assist in the task of running a university.

8. The students who filled the questionnaire on undergraduate relationships generally felt that their mates pressured them too much while a few felt their mates were too immature in their outlook.

9. *Two Thousand Seasons* a novel by Ayi Kwei Armah is one of the few African novels which handles the subject of the Slave Trade.

10. Several students who observed the experiment for the first time opted to study physics as a major.

11. Kweku Kwabena Maame Adwoa you must listen to this story to the end.

12. The University of Cape Coast which looks so beautiful on the master plan is not really as attractive as it was meant to be.

13. Their examinations completed the head of department gave the graduating students a party to celebrate.

14. The workers stopped work early that day the building well painted and the rest of their supplies returned to the stores.

15. I should remember that the porter not the cleaner should be entrusted with these supplies.

16. Being **ponded** was perhaps the second most annoying humiliating experience I have ever had.

17. The unemployed graduate student took over the pen reserved for captured animals and renovated it into an affordable neat appealing and cozy restaurant.

18. She lives at Bantama Kumasi.

19. "I will be home soon" said the man to his son over the phone "and then you can tell me all about it" he concluded.

20. Although it has its benefits development destabilizes people.

Semi-colon (;)

Under the discussion of the uses of the comma, we learnt that one of the uses of the semi-colon is that it separates independent clauses:

> The possession of this handbook matters very little; what must be appreciated is the consequence of mastering what it teaches.
>
> In the first stanza the poet had been suggesting that she could not know this experience if she tried; in the last stanza it is clear that she cannot help but know it.

The other use of the semi-colon is that it separates elements in a series when some of the elements already contain commas.

> I spoke to the President of our association, who assured me that she, like other members of the caucus, disapproved; I notified the treasurer who had not been present during the discussion; and I wrote an account of the action as an appendix to the report.

Use the semi-colon in the sentence before transitional connectives between two main clauses. Some of the common transitional connectives include **also, besides, consequently, furthermore, yet, therefore, likewise, nevertheless** etc.

> He always arrives late at meetings; yet he is always the first to complain that the meetings take too long.
>
> The defendant brought up new evidence; consequently he was set free at the new trial.

Exercises on the Semi-colon

Instructions: insert semi-colons in the appropriate places in these sentences:

1. The bus comes whenever it does the transport officer insists the drivers respect time.

2. The profit or loss pertaining to a particular year will be shown after depreciation has been charged this will present an objective view of the assets on the balance sheet.

3. Helen ignored her sister's advice to become a hairdresser she wanted to be a scientist.

4. Lej Iyasu was excommunicated because he was a libertine his moral standing was highly questionable.

5. We must learn to take care of our lungs cars with faulty exhaust system must be impounded immediately.

6. Ghanaians must seriously consider cremation as an alternative way of disposing of the dead this way the country will save on land and expensive wood.

7. Tro-tros are cheap but they waste too much time private cars are fast but they are too expensive to maintain airplanes are very fast and very expensive.

8. There is nothing wrong with sharing information you have discovered in the library there is everything wrong with behaving as if information should be hoarded.

9. I never have any problems understanding the theories of grammar I always had a hard time using grammar correctly.

10. The journals at this university aim at publishing the research efforts of faculty members they do not have profit as an objective.

Colon (:)

The specific function of the colon is to introduce the material which follows the colon. The material may be a list, a statement, an example, or whatever the earlier part of the sentence has led the reader to expect.

> The sticker on his car read: caution: I drive like you.

> Something terrible happened after matriculation: the student was ponded, while he was wearing the rich kente cloth his father had given him for the occasion.

Use the colon in the place of a comma before a long or formal quotation.

In an earlier poem whose narration of a journey away from life recalls "Our journey had advanced," Emily Dickson had written:

> 'Twas the old – road – through pain –
> That unfrequented – one –
> With many a turn – and thorn –
> That stops – at Heaven –

Exercises on the Colon

Instructions: insert colons where appropriate in the following sentences

1. The writing on the wall said Jesus loves You.

2. The university graduate school has one underlying philosophy to encourage critical reflexive thinking.

3. Acknowledgment of sources or documentation can be done in two ways footnotes or documentation.

4. Kwame Nkrumah declared "Independence now".

5. The telegram read missing you terribly.

Quotation Marks (" " Or ' ')

The double quotation marks are used in the following instances:

> To set off the actual words of a speaker or writer.
>
> In his confusion, Hamlet soliloquized: "To be or not to be, that is the question . . ."
>
> "Allegory," Paul de Man writes, "involves the tendency of the language toward narrative, the spreading out along the axis of an imaginary time in order to give duration to what is, in fact, simultaneous within the subject."
>
> "Why should I be the only one to do the dishes today?" she wailed.

Use the double quotation marks to set off a word or group of words under discussion.

> "Nomenclature" is the word used to facilitate the naming of plants and animals.
>
> In Ghanaian English the word "tea" may refer to actual tea, or coffee or a chocolate drink or indeed to any kind of hot drink.

The title of an article, poem, short story or song is usually acknowledged by using the double quotation marks.

> Boateng, Akwasi, "The uses of the Praise Song" in *Voices of Ghana*, Emefa Addo, ed., Accra, Ghana Publishing Corporation 1992.
>
> John Milton's poem, "On His Blindness" is one of the most moving poems I have ever read.
>
> "No Sweetness Here" is the title of one of Ama Ata Aidoo's short stories.
>
> One of the most popular highlife songs which all the political parties played in their feverish endeavours to gain political power was "Onyame Ehu Wo".

The single quotation mark is used to set off a quotation within the quotation.

> The teacher of religions said, "Today we need to start our discussion with the verse which begins with – 'I was hungry, and you gave me no food'".

Use quotation marks to set off words in a discussion.

> His use of "intelligence quota" does not take culture into account.

> The world "love" means different things to different people.

Use quotation marks for unfamiliar terms.

> In music the climax of the composition is called the "bridge".
> "Freytag's pyramid" describes the classical structure of tragedy.

Use quotation marks for nicknames and epithets.

> His classmates called him "macho" while he was a student.
> "Boom Boom" Mancini died after a boxing bout.

Exercises on the Comma and Quotation Marks

Instruction: insert commas and quotation marks where appropriate in the following sentences.

1. Rosemond Quansah wrote an article titled The nutritional value of *dawa-dawa* which is most revealing.

2. The discussion today is going to focus on ponding.

3. You left your files in my office I told my student whose long essay I am supervising. I wonder if you have been able to carry out the suggestions. Oh she remarked I have been searching everywhere for them.

4. His father calls him sonny at home and his friends call him dangerous.

5. It all depends on what we mean by free and fair elections.

Apostrophe(')

Strictly speaking, the apostrophe is not a mark of punctuation because it does not occur between words as do other forms of punctuation. However, we are including it in this section because it functions more or less as a punctuation mark. Its primary functions are to form the possessive case and to indicate contractions and dropped letters.

Use the apostrophe to form the passive case singular words by adding an 's' to the singular word.

>The candle's glow.
>My daughter's science project.
>Sam's house.

The use of the apostrophe in these phrases indicates that first word possesses the second word, so that the glow belongs to the candle, the science project is owned by my daughter and the house is occupied by someone called Sam.

There are times when the singular word ends with an s or an x as in "boss" and "box" and we may wonder where to place the apostrophe and what to do with the s. Well, place the apostrophe and the **s** in exactly the same place as you would a singular word without an s. For example:

>The box's measurements are wrong.
>My boss's family is really nice.

In certain common cases, as with the word "sake" it is advisable to drop the s even if the noun is singular. Note the following examples:

>for goodness' sake; for convenience' sake; for conscience' sake.

Use the apostrophe to denote an abbreviation in sentence construction as in the following

>It is not so difficult to pass with a good class.
>It's not so difficult to pass with a good class.
>In other words, **it's** is the same as **it is**.

It means **of that thing** as in:

>The tree disperses its seeds by wind (**its** in this sentence refers to the tree, that is, the seeds of the tree). Therefore, there is no such punc-

tuation as **its'** in English.

In a similar case, the word "her" never takes on an apostrophe, so we can never have such a word as "her's". It is always **hers**.

Form the possessive of plural words ending in *s* by adding the apostrophe alone.

> The candles' glow; my daughters' science project; the Sams' house.

Plural nouns which do not end with an s are treated as singular nouns when it comes to adding the apostrophe, as in the following:

> women's rights   children's habits   the fungi's effect

Since there are no words like **womens, childrens** and **fungis,** we cannot have an apostrophe coming after them. In other words it is wrong to write

> womens' right   childrens' habits   the fungi's effect

Avoid piled up possessives in the academic essay; instead, combine the possessive with **of**. Instead of

> My sister's husband's half-brother's mother-in-law's case at the court.

write

> The case at the court involves a relative of my brother-in-law.

Exercises on the Apostrophe

Instructions: insert apostrophes where appropriate in the following sentences:

1. Its so hard to get a relationship going without trust and respect.

2. My two sons favourite toys are cars with remote control.

3. I gave a talk at the Womens Centre on childrens welfare.

4. The lecturers houses are quite close to the campus.

5. His wife's sisters are very gracious.

Question Mark (?)

The question mark is used for one main purpose: to indicate that the sentence or statement is to be regarded as a question, as in the following:

> Have you been doing the exercises in this hand/work book?
> Are you really telling the truth?
> For sure?

When the question mark is used to separate sentences it is placed in parenthesis and the purpose is to raise doubt about the preceding word or statement as in the following:

> Their greatest concern (?) was the image of this university.
> His generosity (?) was not the least effective.
> I think you and your wife (?) should rationally consider the matter.

Exercises on the Question Mark

Instructions: Place question marks where appropriate in the following sentences:

1. I wonder why the simple business of living should appear so difficult.

2. That film is called "Who is afraid of Virginia Woolfe".

3. Do you sincerely believe in life after death. Are you sure you do.

4. Where does your freedom begin and mine end.

Parenthesis ( )

The parenthesis plays a role quite similar to the comma, the semicolon and the colon in the sense that it is used to separate words from one another. It may be used, like the dash, to set off an explanation, an amplification or a qualification. The parenthesis encloses this extra information which helps to clarify the statement:

> Folklore (in the sense of a people's culture) has been so misused as to acquire a pejorative meaning.

> English words (like weekend and holiday) have invaded the French vocabulary with ease despite the efforts to stop such adulteration.

Exercises on the Parenthesis

Instructions: insert parentheses at the appropriate points in the following sentences:

1. We shall visit Sekondi during the holidays Essikadu to be precise.

2. He loves good food steak and fried rice with vegetables to be precise.

3. His father's hobby was to collect cars expensive and attractive ones when he was not collecting jewelry.

4. The Volta Hotel perched on a hill overlooks the Akosombo dam.

5. The life of Bessie Head 1935–1986 was short but productive.

Full Stop or Period (.)

The full stop or period is used to punctuate the end of a sentence which is not a question, a command or an exclamation.

> I hope you are taking your studies seriously.
> You need to have some extra-curricular activities.

Use the full stop or period to mark formal abbreviations as in the following:

> Titles: Mr., Dr., Lt. Col., Fr., Sr., etc.
> Degrees: B.Sc., M.Ed., Ph.D. etc.
> Days and months: Mon., Tues., Oct., Feb., etc.

Do not use full stops for common abbreviations and acronyms:

> OAU, ECOWAS, UNO, UNESCO, UNDP, NDC, NPP.

Chapter 10

DOCUMENTATION; FOOTNOTES AND BIBLIOGRAPHY

Strictly speaking, documentation is a feature of the research paper, and in the sequel to this handbook we hope to tackle the subject in more detail. However, it is important to remind you of some of the ways in which the sources we use in our essays can be acknowledged. What you are doing at this stage in your studies is basically to discover what others have done in your field of study and what you think about that information; in other words, you are required to do critical thinking.

When you discover a book or an article which speaks to an issue in your course and you wish to use that fact in your essay, then it is imperative that you let your reader know where you got that fact from. Certainly, this begs the question – what is to be documented? Usually, commonplace ideas on the subject are not documented because it is near impossible to find the one who first thought up that idea. But when an author has used some facts from his research to support an idea, and you make use of his data or facts, or when you quote, (lift words directly from a source), or when you paraphrase the quotation, then it is only fair to give that author due credit and respect by making the reader aware that those facts are indeed not yours. There is nothing wrong with using material others have thought of; but there is everything wrong with using someone else's facts as your own. Acknowledgment of sources or documentation can be done in two ways: footnotes and bibliography.

Footnotes

Footnotes are useful in helping you to keep the train of thought in your essay without constantly pausing to give evidence to the source of your quotation or close paraphrase. What is usually done is to insert a number above the final letter of the quotation; you keep numbering until you come to the end of your sources – so that in your essay you will have the numbers 1, 2, 3, etc. scattered in there somewhere on the pages, and at the foot of the page, you supply information about that book. If footnote number 1 occurs on page four of your essay, the foot of page four should tell us where that particular quotation or idea is coming from. When you plan to use such a method, you should make sure that there is enough space left at the foot of the page to provide the required information. This advice is particularly important when you have more than a footnote on a page.

Format for the Footnote

When you are supplying information about a source which you have used, you need to be very precise, so that your reader can locate that source if necessary. In order to do this you need to give the following information in the following order:

> name of author, beginning with the first name on the book, title of the book which must be underlined, page number.

The rest of the information about that particular source will have to be provided in a complete bibliography which lists all the material you consulted in the course of your paper; for the time being just the above three items will satisfy the requirement of footnotes.

If your source comes from a journal, magazine or newspaper, the following format is required:

(a) name of author, beginning with the first name in the article
(b) the title of the article, which must be given in quotation marks
(c) the name of the journal, magazine or newspaper, which must be underlined
(d) the number or volume or edition of the journal, magazine or newspaper
(e) date and page number

You must place a comma at the end of each item in the footnote and a full stop at the end. Please keep this little reminder at hand because to enter the footnote without separating the items with commas and ending with a full stop is an error.

Here are examples of two footnotes to illustrate the acknowledgment of a source from a book and a journal:

> BOOK: Ama Ata Aidoo, *No Sweetness Here*, p.34.
>
> JOURNAL: N. Jane Opoku-Agyemang, "To Rise Again: Of Women and Marriage in Mariama Ba's *So Long A Letter, Asemka*, vol. 6, 1989, pp. 60–61.

There are times when you would have quoted twice or more in succession from the same source; when this happens it is not necessary to give the same documentation twice in a row. For the second acknowledgment of source you simply use the word ibid. If you have referred three times in succession to

Ama Ata Aidoo's *No Sweetness Here*, but you have quoted from a different page each time, your footnotes will look like this:

1. Ama Ata Aidoo, *No Sweetness Here*, p.34.
2. *Ibid.*, p.44.
3. *ibid.*, p.47.

You will notice that a full stop comes after ibid., and this is important in showing an abbreviated form. In this particular case ibid. is the abbreviated form of the Latin word "ibidem" which means "in the same place". *Ibid.*, is also always underlined or highlighted by some mechanical means. At other times you may have quoted from two different sources and you would have acknowledged them adequately in a footnote. Then in the course of the paper it becomes important to quote from the first source again. When this happens you still need not repeat the same author, title, etc. all over again. You may proceed like this:

1. Ama Ata Aidoo, *No Sweetness Here*, p.34.
2. Adeola James. *In Their Own Voices African Women Writers Talk*, p.67.
3. Aidoo, p.44.
4. *Ibid.*, p.47.
5. James, p.52.

Using the Explanatory Footnote

Footnoting is not always that straightforward; there will be times when you may need to elaborate, or comment on, or provide additional information which is interesting and important but which may divert attention from the main point you want to discuss at the particular point in your work. When such an occasion arises, you will need to write out an explanatory footnote. It is useful, however, to try to avoid such a method particularly at this state in your studies because if not properly handled it can cause confusion.

Endnotes

Endnotes function in the same way as footnotes, except that the sources are compiled at the end of the entire paper and not at the foot of the page. Sometimes this method is very convenient especially if you are handling your paper as a manuscript and not a typescript. It is important to check with your instructor in order to find out what is required.

Exercises on Footnotes and Endnotes

Write out each of the exercises by using the correct footnote format.

1. An article entitled "Political Changes at the Grassroots Level" written by P. A. Bonsu appeared in *Politics Now and Forever* on February 14, 1993, volume five, page 26.

2. The same article above, same page.

3. A book by Edward, D. Johnson entitled *The Handbook of Good English,* pages 219 to 237.

4. Same as item three above, page 258.

5. Same as item one above, page 28.

6. Journal titled *Much Ado About Everything* containing an article written by H.A. Manso appeared in volume fifteen of *Nothing but the Truth*, page 22.

The Bibliography

The bibliography gives complete information about the sources you have used in your paper. You need to be consistent in the form you choose to present your bibliography in. When we come to discuss the research paper in our next handbook we will have time to present the various acceptable formats for the bibliography. For the time being the following format will do. If in doubt, consult your course instructor.

Unlike footnoting and endnoting which do not require any rigidity in form, the bibliography is very formal. It is important to respect the alphabetical order, and you always need to supply the last name of the author first. If the book has been written by more than one author, the name of the second author is to be written first name first. For example, a book written by Lucy Acheampong and Christine Sackey should be entered this way:

Acheampong, Lucy and Christine Sackey.

If the book has been written by more than two people, you need to enter the first name only and add *"et. al."* which means "and others". For example a book written by Lucy Acheampong, Christine Sackey and Aisha Gyasi will be entered in the following manner:

>Acheampong, Lucy, *et. al.*,

Sometimes it is not very clear as to which is the first name and which is the last, especially when the names come from a culture you do not share or when either name can be used for a first or last name, as in Anthony Clement. When such an occasion presents itself, you should not take it upon yourself to rearrange the name – simply follow what exists at the back of the book.

When the same author has written more than one book, you need not repeat the author's name for each entry. You only need to provide a long dash in the place of the name in all the entries after the first. For example:

>Ngugi wa Thiong'o, *Weep Not Child*
>–   *A Grain of Wheat*
>–   *Petals of Blood*

When an item is so long that it spills over to the next line, you need to indent the second line in such a way as to make the name of the author stand out.

Example:

>Brooks, Cleanth, *The Well Wrought Urn, Studies in the Structure of Poetry*

>Slatoff, Walter J., *With Respect to Readers: Dimensions of Literary Response*

One of the simplest modes of punctuation in the bibliography is to use commas between all the parts and a full top at the end.

When arranging your bibliography on the handwritten page, leave a line between the entries; if the paper is to be typed be sure to remind the typist to type each entry single space, and leave a double space between the entries.

Example:

>MacCabe, Colin, "Realism and the Cinema: Notes on some Brechtian Theses", *Screen*, vol.17, no.2, 1974, pp. 7–27.

>Wood, Frank, *Business Accounting*, vol. 1, London, 1984.

Spradley, James P., & David W. McCurdy, eds., *Conformity and Conflict*, 4th ed., Boston, Little, Brown, 1980.

Please note the placement of details like the place of publication, publisher and date of publication; this information is indispensable to the bibliographical entry. The rest of our discussion on the bibliography will be taken up by showing you one way of recording bibliographic information for different sources.

Books

Book with One Author
Lucas, Henry J., *Introduction to Computers and Information Systems*, New York, Macmillan, 1986.

Book with Two Authors
Eliot, Alfred M., & Bruce R. Voeller, *Basic Biology*, New York, Appleton, 1952.

Book with more than Two Authors
Mussen, Paul., et al., *Psychology: An Introduction*, Lexington, Mass, D.C. Heath, 1973.

Book with Corporate Authorship
Editors of *Women's Writing Today*, Accra, Universities of Ghana Press, 1993.

A Later Edition
Guerin, Wilfred L. et al., *A Handbook of Critical Approaches to Literature*, 3rd ed., New York, Oxford, Oxford University press, 1992.

A Work in more than One Volume
Bloomsbury, Catherine, *Victorian Novelists*, 2 vols., New York, Random House, 1985.

A Work in Translation
Fanon, Frantz, *The Wretched of the Earth*, Trans, **Constance Farrington**, London, Heinemann, 1970.

A Work in a Series
Bergman, Ingmar, *The Seventh Seal*, New York, Simon & Schuster, 1968.

A Book with an Editor
Davis, Carol Boyce & Anne Adams, Eds., *Ngambika: Studies of Women in African Literature*, Trenton, New Jersey, Third World Press, 1986.

A Book with an Author and an Editor
Melville, Herman, *The Confidence Man: His Masquerade*, ed. Hershel Parker, New York, W.W. Norton, 1971.

A Selection from an Edited Anthology or Collection
Gerald, Carolyn F., "The Black Writer and His Role", In *The Black Aesthetic*, ed., Addison Gayle, Jr., Garden City, New York, Anchor-Doubleday, 1972.

A Reprint
Kane Cheikh Hamidou, *Ambiguous Adventure*, New York, Walker & Company, 1973, rpt., New York, Macmillan, 1969.

Magazines, Periodicals, Newspapers

An Article in a Periodical
Yeboah, Anthony, "Safety in the Laboratory", *Ghana Journal of Science*, 18, Sept 1990, pp. 42–57.

An Article in a Magazine
Katz, Donald R., "Drawing Fire: Cartoonist Bill Maudlin and His 35-year Fight for Truth, Justice, and the American Way", *Rolling Stone,* 4 Nov., 1976, pp. 52–54, 56, 58, 60, 89.

An Article in a Magazine
"The Youth and the Charismatic Church" *Uhuru,* 22 Nov., 1992, p.3.

An Article from a Newspaper
"Ghanaians Protest the Death Penalty'" *Our Choice,* 2 June 1986, Sec 1, p.5, col. 4.

Encyclopedias and Almanacs

An Unsigned Article from an Encyclopedia
"Griot" *The New Africa Encyclopedia,* 1990 ed.

An Article from an Encyclopedia
Dickson, K. B. "Ghana", *Encyclopedia Britannica*, 1970 ed.

Bulletins, Pamphlets, and Government Documents
Train the Trainer, Cape Coast, Ghana Project on Institutional Renewal through the Improvement of Teaching, 1988.

Unpublished Dissertations and Theses
Asamoa, Kwadwo, "Ngugi wa Thiong'o as a literary Critic"' Diss., University of Cape Coast 1990.

Films and Television Programms
Allen, Woody, dir., *Manhattan*, With Woody Allen, Diane Keaton, Michael Murphy, Meryl Streep and Anne Byrne.

Osofo Dadzie, Writ, Nanabanyin Wattemberg, G.B.C., 1 Oct. 1975.

Plays and Concerts
Martin Owusu, dir., *The Blinkards,* By Kobina Sekyi, With Evans Hunter, Performing Arts Theater, 21 February 1984.

Sagoe, Kobina, cond., University of Cape Coast Orchestra, Symphony Hall, Cape Coast, 9 July 1986.

Records
Coltrane, John, *A Love Supreme*, Motown, SD 5057, 1960.

Interviews
Soyinka, Wole, Telephone Interview, 24 May 1986.

Exercises on the Bibliography

Instructions: arrange the following in the correct bibliographic format:

1. In 1968, Abraham Clapham edited a book called Black Voices: An Anthology of Afro-American Literature. The book was published by the New American Library in New York.

2. There is an interesting article, in Southern Folklore Quarterly, volume, 24, published in 1960. This article, titled The New Orlenas Voodoo Ritual Dance and its Twentieth Century Survivals, was written by John Q. Anderson on pages 135–43.

3. Et in Arcadia Ego: Representation, Death, and the Problem of Boundary in Emily Dickinson is the title of an article written by Sharon Cameron. This article is included in the collection of essays called American Women Writers which Harold Bloom edited and which was published in 1986 by Chelsea House Publishers in New York.

4. The fifth volume of The History of Science Clinics in Ghana, published in 1988 in Cape Coast by Cape Coast University Press, was written by Harriet Idun Acquah, Dora Edu-Buandoh, Rachel Amable and Ivy Owusu.

5. In 1990 Mariama Ba's novel, So Long A Letter, was translated by Y. S. Boafo and published in Accra by Nsamankow Press.

6 A pamphlet entitled Life On Earth was published in Kumasi by the University of Science and Technology Press on November 19, 1987.

One of the best ways of getting used to the bibliographical format is to make it a habit of writing out the correct bibliographical format for every book and article of which you make use. You may begin by looking at your bookshelf now or at a later time and writing out the bibliography of the books which you own.

BIBLIOGRAPHY

Barnet, Sylvan and Stubbs, Marcia, 1975. *Barnet and Stubb's Practical Guide To Writing,* Boston, Little, Brown and Company.

Crews, Frederick, 1974. *The Random House Handbook*, New York, Random House.

Gillespie, Sheena, *et. al.,* 1989. *The Writer's Craft: A Process Reader,* Glenview, Illinois, Scott, Foesman & Co.

Knodt, Ellen A., 1986. *Writing: Process and Purpose,* New York, Macmillan Publishing Company.

Leedy, Paul D., 1963. *Read with Speed and Precision,* New York, McGraw-Hill Book Company.

Muller, Gilbert, H. (ed.) 1988. *The McGraw-Hill Reader,* 3rd ed., New York, McGraw-Hill Inc.

Perrin, Robert, 1987. *The Beacon Handbook,* Boston, Houghton Mufflin Company.

Webb, Suzanna S., 1986. *Harbrace College Handbook*, 10th ed., San Diego, Harcourt Brace Jovanovich, Publishers.

www.ingramcontent.com/pod-product-compliance
Lightning Source LLC
Chambersburg PA
CBHW070945230426
43666CB00011B/2563